THE NEW COMPLETE SAINT BERNARD

The Statue of Saint Bernard of Menthon and "Pain de Sucre," elev. 9517 feet.

The New Complete
SAINT BERNARD

by

Milo Denlinger
Professor Albert Heim
Mrs. Henry H. Hubble
Gerda Umlauff
Joe Stetson

Edited and Expanded
by
E. Georgean Raulston,
Rex Roberts
and others

1973
Fourth Edition

2nd Printing

HOWELL BOOK HOUSE INC.
· 730 Fifth Avenue
New York, N.Y. 10019

Richards Studio

Cherryacres Lisolotte, owned by Eve Rankin.

Printed in U.S.A.   ISBN 0-87605-271-5

Contents

Foreword 7

Foreword to the 1963 Revision 9

Acknowledgements 11

The Hospice of St. Bernard 15
    Climate . . . The Monks . . . The Dogs . . . The Hospice Today

The Crossing of the Alps by Napoleon 31

The History of the St. Bernard Dog
    by Professor Albert Heim 37

St. Bernard Breeders in Switzerland 1873 to 1904 45

St. Bernards in Switzerland into the 1970's 50

St. Bernards in Germany
    with research by Gerda Umlauff 55

St. Bernards in England 81

Early American Breeders 85

The St. Bernard in America to Mid-Century
    by Mrs. Henry H. Hubble 101
    Introduction to America . . . Founding of the Breed Club . . . Breed
    Progress 1932-1945 . . . Importance of Smooth Breeding Stock . . .
    Leading Saint Bernards in the United States . . . East Coast Breeders
    . . . Midwest Breeders . . . West Coast Breeders . . . Historical Note
    from the Editors

The St. Bernard in North America into the 1970's 122
    Breed Clubs . . . The International View . . . The Show Ring . . .
    Importing . . . Smooth or Rough? . . . Conclusion . . . Recommended
    Reading

Interpretation of the Standard 139
    General Analysis . . . Functional Analysis . . . Specific Analysis . . .
    Additional Analysis . . . Recent Developments . . . The Saint in
    Pictured Motion

Official Standard of the St. Bernard 161

Special Problems of Giant Dogs
  by Joe Stetson 167
  The Growth Pattern of a Giant Dog
A Week-End with the Saints 185
  Observations on Type ... A Dedicated Fancy
The Saint Fancier's Forum 191
  How Can I Find the Right Puppy? ... What Does a Puppy Cost? ...
  What Does It Cost to Feed a Saint Bernard? ... Will He Bite
  Me? ... Does He Have a Good Disposition ... Is the Saint a Good
  Watchdog? ... When Should Training Begin? ... How Can I Keep
  Him Out of Trouble?
The Saint in Action 211
The St. Bernard Club of America National
  Specialty Show, 1972 216

Foreword

THIS edition of *The New Complete Saint Bernard* brings the reader up to date on what is happening on the contemporary national and international scene. International friendships and collaborations are beginning. The outgrowth of an intense search for fine specimens world-wide has led to more standardization. We have tried to include as many of the fine historical archetypes as possible with their contemporary equals throughout this edition.

History cannot be changed. The revisions present new materials as they have become applied to the Saint Bernard, many new photographs and an up-grading of technical data. The best of the previous edition has remained in this edition.

As well as offering photographs and cold facts, we have tried to add touches of "heart." The greater majority of the breed is, after all, owned by those whose better emotions have been touched by the beauty and dignity of this great breed.

The Saint is the ultimate dog. If I may repeat the words of the late Rex Roberts, "... and owners have grasped the vision of the ultimate dog: as big as canine structure will permit, as heavy of bone and body as his work requires, as gentle and yet indestructible as we hope all the members of our family will be."

It is said that no man says anything but there is someone who thinks he could have said it better. The above quotation could not be improved upon.

Let the message ring out: "All has not been done but the patterns are drawn and work continues."

E. GEORGEAN RAULSTON

7

A group of Saint Bernards with their master at the Hospice in Switzerland.

Foreword to the 1963 revision

THIS edition of The Complete Saint Bernard is a major revision of the original book written by Milo Denlinger and others, and published in 1952. The historical portions remain substantially unchanged. Discussion of the breed as it exists today has been almost entirely revised, in order to keep pace with the increasing number of Saint Bernard fanciers, and with the widespread improvement they have created in the individual representatives of the breed.

Since the Saint Bernard was first recognized as a breed, there have been good, and great, representatives thereof. Along with the good ones, there have been many of the not so good. A breed so large, magnificent, surrounded by legend and beset by press agentry, true and untrue, and endowed with a size which magnifies every virtue and fault out of all proportion, is bound to have had trouble in achieving a definition as to what constitutes a good Saint Bernard.

This difficulty is now approaching resolution. Though it is neither cheap nor easy to have a Saint Bernard around the house, in the sense that it is neither cheap nor easy to have a wife, husband, son or daughter, the Saint has become a member of the family, a task for which he is well equipped.

During the past few years, Saint Bernard breeders and owners have grasped the vision of the ultimate dog, as big as canine structure will permit, as heavy of bone and body as his work requires, as gentle and yet indestructible as we hope all the members of our family will be.

We thank all Saint Bernard breeders and owners who have contributed to the support of this growing vision.

REX ROBERTS

The Hospice in winter.

Acknowledgements

Acknowledgements carried over from the first edition are:

To the Hospice of Saint Bernard and to the Saint Bernard Club of Switzerland for information furnished and for the use of illustrations.

To Miss Gerda Umlauff of Hamburg, Germany, for research in the Swiss and German history of the breed.

To Mrs. Henry Hubble, for the chapter on Saint Bernards in America.

Acknowledgements for the 1963 revision are:

First, to many secretaries of area Saint Bernard clubs who gathered information, names, and pictures relating to the modern fancy. Space permits the inclusion of only a small part of this material. The rest is being kept on file for possible use in later editions. Club secretaries who contributed significantly include:

Mrs. William Buell; Box 134, Canoga Park, Calif. (Southern California)

Mrs. Eugene Coulter; 17645 West 44th Ave., Golden, Colo. (Rockies)

Ulrich Engler; 13418 Second Ave., East Cleveland, Ohio (Ohio)

Mrs. Roy Gresham; 838 Lehigh Ave., Union, N. J. (Northern New Jersey)

Mrs. Harold Holmes; 434 Elm St., Bridgewater, Mass. (New England)

Mrs. Frank Lake; 1101 Laurel Road, Beverly, N. J. (Eastern)

Mrs. William McCausland; 5920 Bernhard Ave., Richmond, Calif. (Pacific Coast)

Mrs. Richard Seaman; R.R. 2, Markham, Ont. (Ontario)

Mrs. E. P. Wade; Box 151, West Chicago, Ill. (Northern Illinois)

Officers of the Saint Bernard Club of America made extensive contributions. Of special value were the information files maintained by the secretary, Edward A. Poor, R.D. 1, Acton, Mass. Mr. Poor also contributed lists, names, dates, and editorial advice. Other SBCA officers who assisted were Laurence Powell, Paul Wallbank, Richard Jackson, Boyd Shonkwiler, and Paul Cocanour.

Saint specialty judges Norman F. Keller and Dr. Henry E. Wedig, Sr., gave much time and thought to the problems of clarification, and made specific suggestions in writing. Mrs. Hubble once again must be thanked for her experienced suggestions and criticisms.

Also thanked are those individuals who, acting by request, made significant contributions. They include C. M. Cawker, Ed Dodd, Mary Lou Dube, Joan Edge, Cordelia Englund, Grace Harvey, Beatrice Knight, and William Roberts.

Professional photographers whose recent work was solicited for the revision include William Brown, Edward Harrison, Robert Jollimore, Frank Mazanec, Ruth Robbins, Evelyn Shafer, Paul Winick, Dave Wurzel, and Dick Yemma.

Many more secretaries, the record-keepers of a growing fancy, contributed to the 1966 edition. A partial list includes:

Mrs. Nancy Crane, Wilderness Lane, High Ridge, Missouri (Greater St. Louis)

Marian Sharp, Mine Hill, Dover, N. J. (Northern New Jersey)

Mrs. Jean Cox, 21 Partridge Lane, Agincourt, Ontario (Ontario)

Penny Little, 23596 Candace, Rockwood, Michigan (Michigan)

Mrs. Kaye Wessar, RD 3, Anderson, Indiana (Central Indiana)

Pat Thibedeau, RD 2, Antioch, Illinois (Northern Illinois)

Patricia Wiggins, 816 Sunkist Parkway, Minneapolis, Minn. (Minnesota)

James Yost, 501 W. 70th Place, Denver, Colorado (Rockies)

Photographers who contributed extensively were Jarvis Hunt, Jr., and James Howlett. Other contributors are literally too numerous to mention, but thanks anyway.

Acknowledgements for the 1973 revision:

The Secretary of the Saint Bernard Club of America, Mrs. Marion Sharp, contributed extensively as did other officials of that club: Mr. Edward Poor, Mrs. Viola Wade, Mrs. Carol Pyle, Winifred Martin with her fine art work, Beatrice Knight, Dr. George Wessar, and Shirlie Cox.

I thank the Specialty Judges with whom I discussed ideas of a technical nature: Merc Cresap, Albert de la Rie, Judith Goodin, Ann Gallup, O. M. Capodice, Hans Zimmerli, Dr. George Wessar and his charming wife, Kaye.

Also thanked are the many individuals who, acting upon request, made significant contributions: Mrs. Alvin Holt, Mr. C. M. Cawker, Betty Roberts, Lorraine Raap, Ann Golden, Dr. Antonio Morsiani and Mrs. Caroline Roberts who generously helped with ideas and brought to me the materials her late husband, Rex Roberts, had accumulated.

A special thank you to the many dedicated fanciers with whom I have discussed the breed, who forwarded ideas, suggestions, materials and photographs to be used in this edition. All could not be named, but one should be: Father Cretton of the Hospice.

To the hundreds of fanciers who forwarded materials and photographs that could not be used due to space limitations, I thank you.

To the many hard-working club secretaries all over the world who have gathered pictures, membership lists and information to be included in this edition, my thanks.

Those who offered great encouragement and friendship are my husband, David B. Raulston; Herman Peabody; Gloria Wallin; Mr. and Mrs. Ron Hedien; Dr. and Mrs. Herbert Zeitlin; Dr. and Mrs. Walter Tice; and Mrs. Peter McNulty.

13

Another view of the Hospital of Great Saint Bernard and "Pain de Sucre."

The Hospice of St. Bernard

LOCATED more than 8,000 feet high in the Swiss Alps, the Hospice of the Great St. Bernard is one of the most highly elevated human habitations in Europe. As it sits in somber solitude, surrounded by the towering masses of snow covered mountain peaks, the Hospice through the centuries has remained what its name implies: a symbol of hospitality. Kings and beggars alike have found shelter and protection from the raging elements within its sturdy walls and the good deeds of the monks and their dogs have been highly praised in many languages.

Numerous legends surround the origin of the Hospice as no documents are available that contain the facts of its founding. The most credible story is that the original Hospice, a humble structure of several cell-like rooms, was founded in the 10th Century by Archdeacon Bernard of the St. Augustine Cathedral. Archdeacon Bernard was originally the son of a wealthy noble family which had its residence at the Castle of Menthon near the Lake of Annecy (Savoy). Upon completion of his education in Paris, Bernard began to teach theology, but his father requested his immediate return to Menthon. There he had, in the traditional manner, selected a bride for him.

15

Bernard returned to Menthon but, contrary to his father's wishes, decided to remain in the theological profession. He fled to Aosta (Italy) where he entered the St. Augustine Cathedral as a Canon Regular and after the death of Archdeacon Peter became Preacher and Archdeacon of the Cathedral.

The Mons Jovis Pass, at which the Hospice of St. Bernard is located, had received its name from a temple that the Roman Emperors had built on the summit of the pass and dedicated to their god, Jupiter Penninus. At that time the pass was one of the principal roads connecting Switzerland with Italy. It was used primarily for commercial purposes, but several great armies of medieval emperors and, in 1800, that of Napoleon, used it to their advantage. As the Tomb of the Apostles in Rome induced a constant movement of salvation-seeking Christians, this road became also one of the main arteries for the Italian-bound pilgrimages. Merchants and pilgrims preferred the summer months for their mountain traverse, when daylight prevailed longer and the creeks were shallow and easy to cross. However, they were unable to foresee the dangers awaiting them as they proceeded.

Upon reaching the summit the travelers often were subjected to robberies and attacks by the heathen inhabitants of the mountains. These robbers were some of the wild Saracens who after a reign of terror and destruction had been driven out of the valleys and lived savagely in mountain caves. They cleverly took advantage of the mythological superstitions of that time and established their main hideout in the ruins of the old Mons Jovis temple from which they approached the exhausted travelers as threatening "ghosts."

Archdeacon Bernard, in his efforts to eliminate the danger of robberies, went to preach to the heathen and finally succeeded in converting them to Christianity. He realized the need for a shelter at the mountain pass and in 1050 inaugurated the building of the Hospice. It was a simple structure resembling one of the refuge huts frequently found in the mountains. Bernard's parents, who had been grief-stricken since his departure, visited him at the Hospice and donated a large part of their wealth toward its completion and maintenance. St. Bernard died at 85 years of age, having served as an Archdeacon for 40 years.

The Hospice served its purpose well. In the *Pilgrim's Guide of Saint Iago di Compostela*, printed in France in 1139, it was spoken

A monk and his dogs at the Hospice.

of as one of the three great hospices in the world. We read: "The welfare of the poor rests on three strong pillars: the Hospice of Jerusalem, the Hospice of Mons Jovis and the Hospice of St. Christina at the Somport (Pyrenees). These Hospices were built at locations at which there is great need for them. They are sacred places, houses of the Lord, indispensable for the welfare of the holy pilgrims, the rest of the needy, the consolation of the ailing, peace of soul for the dead and assistance to the living."

During the centuries the Hospice received its operating funds from donations by English and German royalty, the Popes and other ecclesiastical dignitaries as well as neighboring bishops and clerics and the Family of Savoy, as they realized the importance of this institution. Pilgrims and merchants who had enjoyed the monks' hospitality demonstrated their gratitude by building other, smaller hospices which they gave to the monastery of St. Bernard. With its steadily increasing riches in lands and money, in the thirteenth century the Hospice was able to have its buildings enlarged considerably.

The Hospice operated under an independent administrative system and the Prior's authority in financial, as well as disciplinary matters, was generally recognized. As the Provost, who had final authority in all matters, resided at the mother-house of the Order in Martigny, the privilege of self-administration was grossly abused by the Priors as well as the monks. Provost Jean d'Acres in 1417 attempted to counteract this abuse by setting up strict regulations for monks and Priors in which he demanded abstinence from worldly sins such as dancing, drinking, hunting, carrying arms and wearing fancy clothes. He also requested that a superior be appointed to teach and supervise the monks, as many of them were illiterate and were not even able to administer the holy sacraments. However, little consideration was shown these regulations and they were soon forgotten after Provost Jean d'Acres retired in 1438. The new Provosts, who were elected by the House of Savoy, had little regard for the Hospice's welfare. They wasted its money and went so far as to sell properties belonging to the Hospice.

In 1555 a disastrous fire swept over the Hospice, destroying the roofs and to a large extent the upper walls. For three years the monks were forced to live under the most pitiful and primitive conditions before permission was granted to perform the necessary repair

18

"They always want to take my picture."
A puppy at the Hospice du Grand Saint Bernard.

Approaching the *Cantine de Proz*, after travelling through the forests, one still finds a guest house, where travellers can rest, in a valley well-adapted to pasture lands.

work. The first repairs consisted of clearing the rubbish, rebuilding part of the destroyed upper walls and building strong supports for the front of the building. The monks' room, as well as the church, received a new whitewash and the roofs were weighted down with large rocks and stone plates.

The Great St. Bernard, as the mountain was called from then on, seems to have held some kind of fortification. A sketch made in 1626 of the Church and the Hospice reveals part of an ancient parapet south of the buildings. Apparently, a crenelled barrier blocked the pass from the Swiss side and was connected with the Hospice buildings. Another battlement, similar to the parapet blocking the Valley of St. Themy on the Italian side of the mountain, seems to have been at the Plan de Jupiter. In 1476 this stronghold was the scene of bloody battles between the troops of the Count of Challant and the Valais soldiers. According to the legend, the old mortuary (which is still standing) was then built to take care of the enormous number of casualties of the battle in the Combe des Morts.

During the seventeenth century the Hospice was completely remodeled and a new chapel added. The Bishop of Sitten, Adrian VI von Riedmatten, personally performed the consecration of the beautiful little building. Toward the end of the eighteenth century, Provost Ludwig Anton Ludder added the St. Ludwigs Spital on the northern side of the pass to the buildings of the Hospice.

Numerous priors were in charge of the Hospice in succession during medieval time. Most of them had the welfare of the Hospice at heart, others their own financial gain in mind. There was a constant struggle between the constitutionists who duly obeyed the fundamental laws of the congregation and the anti-constitutionists who failed to live according to their vows. In 1752 Pope Benedict XIV passed the "bull de separatione," a papal letter according to which all property on the Swiss side belonged to the orders of St. Mauritius and Lazarus. The anti-constitutionists were made Sardinian subjects, given the Valais property and left in charge of the Great St. Bernard Hospice with the stipulation that the monks were to elect their own provosts. However, this was a very unfortunate solution and caused the Hospice large losses in land, money and personnel. Most of the monks returned to the valleys.

The Hospice had hardly recuperated from the consequences of the separation when the Canton of the Lower Valais declared its

20

The Sanctuary of the Church which was built by the Master-Mason Jean-Antoine
Marcoz, of Brissogne, and consecrated in 1698 by Adrian VI of Riedmatter,
Bishop of Sitten. The choir stall dates back to the year 1681.

21

independence and started a chain of political events at the end of which was the fall of the old Helvetian Confederation and the invasion of Switzerland by French troops.

Climate

Rock, snow, and ice are the principal elements in the vicinity of the Hospice. No vegetation is able to withstand the extremely cold and most undesirably variable climate. Some lone, weather-beaten pines clinging to the rocks about 2,000 feet below the pass are the last sign of organic life. Even during the months of July and August, frost occurs daily and the monks know of only approximately twenty days annually that are free from frost and ice. The small lake in front of the buildings, which constitutes the boundary between Switzerland and Italy, is often frozen the year round. Many of the travelers, arriving at the Hospice after having been exposed to the sub-zero temperatures for the long hours of their ascent, suffer frozen extremities. This applies particularly to the seasonal laborers crossing the pass insufficiently clothed. Frequently it becomes necessary for the monks to supply these people with warm clothing, as well as to provide dry clothes for all comers that have encountered drenching rains, snow storms, or the dankness of the mountain fog.

Many of the monks' experiences tell of the unpredictable weather conditions on the mountain. Travelers starting out on a bright, sunny morning may after a few hours be overcome by violent snow storms that not only eliminate visibility but, accompanied by falling temperatures, cause the snow to freeze on hair and clothing.

During the winter months the snow reaches a depth of thirty feet and causes the Hospice to become almost completely isolated. The tremendous winds to which the buildings are continually exposed change during the winter months into treacherous snow storms. A few people, most of them laborers seeking employment in the warmer Italy, venture across the mountain during the winter. It is a perilous undertaking, as the way is partially covered by large snow drifts and the passage at the summit becomes almost inaccessible. Posts that are connected with a strong rope have been anchored in the rock to guide the traveler over the steepest part on the summit.

One of the greatest dangers the traveler may encounter is the avalanche—a mass of ice, rock, and snow, which viciously thunders from the cliffs carrying with it destruction and certain death. Even those familiar with the dangers of the mountains are not always able to escape. Only recently three of the monks were buried by an avalanche while they were searching for lost travelers.

The Monks

Approximately fifteen of the seventy members of the Order of St. Augustine reside at the Hospice. The monks are selected from their mother-house at Martigny for service at the Hospice at the age of eighteen and twenty years. Particular attention is paid to the monks' physical condition in selecting them for service at the Hospice. While monks of excellent constitution have been able to withstand the undesirable climate for longer than fifteen years, others have averaged only twelve years. Almost all of the monks continually residing at the Hospice acquire ailments of the rheumatic type and heart conditions.

Under the supervision of the Prior, three monks perform duties as Master of the Novices, Sacristan, and Host to the Travelers, while a fourth one is in charge of the financial and economic details. Until recently, the older monks at the Hospice taught student priests in the fields of philosophy, literature, history and theology. These educational functions have now been transferred to a Hospice-owned farm at Encone, near Riddes.

The Provost of the Hospice carries the insignias, miter and crosier of a Bishop as first bestowed upon the Provosts of the Hospice by the Pope in 1762.

Brothers of the Order of St. Augustine under the supervision of a Prior also serve the Hospice at the Simplon Pass and nine different Church communities in the valleys.

The Dogs

The dogs of the Great St. Bernard which have been bred, raised and trained by the monks for the past four centuries, have remained one of the main attractions of the Hospice. They are powerfully built dogs of fawn or mahogany color with white markings. Their heads are impressively large and their noble expression gives them an air of dignity. Even though a variety of long haired dogs exists, a short, dense coat is preferred as it does not interfere with the dogs' work in the snow.

The manifold stories relating the rescue of snow-bound travelers by these dogs have added much to their glamour and legendary reputation. The first indication of their existence is a painting by the Neapolitan Salvator Rose of the seventeenth century. Many contradictory views have been expressed regarding the origin of these dogs. It is assumed that they result from cross-breedings of English Hounds and Spaniels, and there is also some legendary belief that they stem from a mating of a Great Dane and a Valais Alpine female. Another assumption is that the St. Bernard dog originates from a large type of hound which the Romans used in their military establishments or that it is a cross of Bulldogs and Pyrenean sheep dogs.

Twelve or fifteen dogs are usually kept at the Hospice and trained for rescue work. The training requires approximately two years and the older and more experienced dogs aid in the training of the younger ones. During the dangerous winter months the monks, accompanied by some of the dogs, used to leave the Hospice every morning and search the pass for exhausted or lost travelers. On occasions the dogs were sent out by themselves and frequently located snow-bound travelers whom they guided safely to the Hospice.

One of the most miraculous rescues was performed by Old Barry, one of the best specimens ever bred at the Hospice. As the story goes, Barry found a small boy in the snow and by some mysterious means got him to climb on his back and carried him to safety. With Barry's death in 1814 the Hospice lost one of its most famous guide and rescue dogs. During the twelve years of his life he had rescued more than 40 persons and his work has not been equalled since. The Museum of Berne preserved and mounted him and today, after more than one century, he is still the object of respectful admiration. The monks honor Barry by naming after him those dogs bred at the Hospice that are beautiful in appearance and of excellent character and ability.

Among the deeds of rescue well remembered in the history of the Hospice is one which occurred in the winter of 1874. Some Italian laborers insisted on crossing the pass on a most dangerous and unpredictable day. As the monks felt it was their duty to assist the travelers, seven of them and one dog accompanied and guided this

24

group of eight persons. After three hours of strenuous climbing in the quickly falling snow, a huge avalanche fell, burying beneath it three of the monks, five of the Italians and the dog. The remainder of the party immediately and fiercely began to dig and search and was able to free five of the victims. The dog, which had freed itself, returned to the Hospice and by its excited behavior informed the Superior of the accident. A rescue party was sent out immediately and for several hours worked laboriously at freeing the persons buried under the avalanche. Unfortunately, the victims had been exposed to sub-freezing temperature so long that they died shortly after being found.

Amazing is the ability of the dogs to discover lost persons even though they are covered by a thick blanket of snow. In 1907 a lone traveler was overtaken by a sudden snow storm. As he had fallen down from exhaustion, the quickly falling snow covered him completely, wiping out his tracks. A rescue party was sent out; and the dog, immediately picking up the scent, led the party to the snow covered victim.

The monks value the service of their dogs very highly and seldom leave the Hospice without them. The dogs easily find their way back to the Hospice by their instinct while the human eye is often unable to penetrate the quickly descending mountain fog.

Even though the dogs are of a sturdy, hardy constitution, their life span is reduced to about ten years by the severe climate. Like their masters, they suffer from rheumatic and heart diseases as well as asthma, as they increase in age.

True to the tradition of the Hospice, the monks have continued to breed these fine dogs even though their services are no longer needed. The Hospice is now easily accessible by automobile and the dangers formerly encountered by the lone traveler on foot are greatly reduced, if not completely eliminated.

The Hospice Today

The Simplon Tunnel (built from 1898 to 1905) now connecting Switzerland and Italy, worms its way $12\frac{1}{4}$ miles through the mountains northeast of the Great St. Bernard Pass. In seven years, human ingenuity has converted the formerly perilous mountain traverse of several days' duration into a pleasant, smooth half-hour trip. However, it has also robbed the passage of its glamour and romance, the Hospice of its purpose, and deprived the traveler of an experience unexcelled in grandeur and impressiveness. No longer need the traveler exert himself in the strenuous ascent, exposed to the hazards of sudden snow storms, avalanches and freezing temperatures; but no longer, also, will he enjoy the grand and wild scenery and the sublime feeling of closeness to eternity inspired by the loneliness of the ice-bound mountains.

Lacking the picturesque loveliness of many other mountain passes, the Great St. Bernard impresses one with its rugged panorama and the massive proportions of the surrounding mountains. Until the end of the nineteenth century the Hospice was the only sign of humanizing influence in this barren canyon. With the completion of a road in 1890, however, the pass became easily accessible. The road has been so improved that it is now travelled by thousands of motorists annually who reach the Hospice in several hours' drive from Martigny. This, however, applies only to the summer months, as during the winter months the road remains closed on account of the danger of avalanches and snow drifts. As the last part of the road is too narrow to permit traffic from both directions, upgoing traffic is restricted to the morning hours, and descending traffic, to the afternoon of each day.

The road now available has also eased considerably the burden of transporting supplies to the Hospice. The countless travelers as well as the monks require large quantities of food to be stocked at the Hospice during the winter months. These supplies were formerly carried up the small path by horses or mules in a laborious ascent. A herd of nearly one hundred cattle and a large flock of sheep enable the Hospice to keep in stock considerable quantities of smoked mutton and salted beef, which in recent years has been frequently supplemented by fresh meat.

The buildings, consisting of the Hospice with connecting Chapel, the St. Ludwigs Spital and the old mortuary, though massive stone structures, seem dwarfed as they huddle against the masses of naked rock rising behind them to a height of 9,400 feet. The Chapel, in which the monks sing Mass daily and perform their hourly prayers, is one of the greatest attractions. Built in the seventeenth century, it still contains its original murals and choir stalls of beautifully carved walnut wood. In the Chapel the Tomb of General Desaix is reminiscent of the battle of Marengo in 1800 when Napoleon defeated the Austrians in Italy.

26

During the years, representatives of all creeds, ranks and religions have gathered in the large entrance hall of the Hospice and decorated it with the tokens of their gratitude. A message of gratitude to Napoleon was inscribed on the wall by the people of the Lower Valais who through him had gained their independence. The piano which King Edward VII presented to the Hospice is also displayed here.

A museum, containing countless objects of great value and interest, occupies the ground floor. The monks have assembled remarkable collections of insects and stones, and they, as well as antique coins, votive tablets and statues discovered at the site of the old Mons Jovis temple, are now on display at the museum.

The west wing of the house is occupied by the monks and not open to the public. The upper floors contain the guest rooms which are simple and clean and contain from one to four beds.

One of the most valuable assets is the library in the loft of the main building. More than 30,000 volumes, some of them hand-written and hand-pressed, make up this marvelous collection of both antique and recent editions in many languages.

With a capacity of 400 beds in its approximately 100 rooms, the Hospice has often accommodated more than 500 overnight guests by converting hallways and the dining hall into sleeping quarters. On occasions like this, all of the monks assist in the preparation and serving of meals and other chores necessary to provide a comfortable stay for the transients. The Hospice does not operate on the basis of a hotel but in accordance with the principles of a religious order. As it was built in the eleventh century for the "welfare of the needy and for the rest of the pilgrims" it still serves this purpose to some extent by giving shelter and food to those in need of it. Everyone who so desires has access to the Hospice. Upon ringing the door bell he will be welcomed by the Father Aumoniér who receives with equal cordiality all guests regardless of nation, rank, or religion.

Unfortunately, curious and thoughtless tourists have greatly abused the monks' generous hospitality; and it is now limited to the truly needy travelers, who are permitted to stay one night during the summer months and as long as necessary during the winter months. (A hotel opposite the Hospice has facilities for 180 overnight guests. It is open the year round.)

Approximately one half of the the 20,000 persons annually visiting the Hospice are Italians, 6,000 or more are Swiss, approximately 2,000 are British tourists, and the remainder are composed of members of all nations of the world. Most of the Italians crossing the pass are needy people or workers in search of employment. They cross the St. Bernard in spring to work during the summer months in Swiss valleys and return to Italy in the fall.

British, German, and Italian royalty have enjoyed the hospitality of the monks. Queen Victoria of England, who spent one night at the Hospice, later presented it with her portrait. At the age of eighteen years, the Prince of Wales, later King Edward VII, was guest of the monks. Upon his departure from the Hospice the Prince was presented with a beautiful St. Bernard puppy. The Prince was deeply upset when the puppy died before the royal party ever reached the valley. Soon after his arrival in England, the Prince repaid the monks' hospitality by presenting the Hospice with a piano, and later, when he became King of England, he had another piano shipped to them. In 1883 King Edward's sister, the late Empress Fredericke of Germany, also visited the Hospice with her husband, the Crown Prince. Frequent visitors during the summer months were the King and Queen of Italy, who traveled by automobile from Aosta.

Saint Bernards from the kennels, Zwinger Zwing-Uri, Flüelen, Switzerland.

28

It seems that the monks' hospitality is enjoyed not only by mankind but by all of the Lord's creation. Twice annually, the swallows on their flights to and from the South rest at the Hospice. As soon as the first ones are noticed, the monks open wide all windows for the graceful little birds to enter. They remain quietly in the building and even permit the monks to caress them. As soon as the weather permits, they are on their way again, chirping a song of thanks to their hosts.

Through the installation of a telephone the Hospice is now in a position to inform those starting their ascent of the weather conditions in the upper regions. On the other hand, the monks can now receive word of travelers approaching so that they may be on the lookout for them in foul weather. Coach service is now provided from Martigny during the months of July and August, and tourists are able to reach the Hospice by automobile, though the trip is time-consuming and arduous.

Some years ago the Hospice was threatened by undesirably large and noisy crowds of tourists. Fortunately, the rugged remoteness of the setting and its difficulty of access soon persuaded the casual tourist to seek his amusement elsewhere. Although a small hotel is now available through part of the year, the serious-minded visitor is content with the sense of austerity and dedication.

At the time of the writing of this present revision the breeding of Saint Bernards continues at the Hospice. The principal purposes of this work now are love of the breed and the continuation of a grand tradition.

Napoleon with his army, scaling the Alps in May 1800.

The Crossing of the Alps
by Napoleon

T HE crossing of the Alps in 1800 which won Napoleon the admiration of his contemporaries was so great an accomplishment that even in our days of modern warfare it impresses us.

At Dijon, France, General Berthier was put in command of the army which he later led to victory at Marengo. Captain Coignet, an old warrior, relates the details of the mountain traverse of his unit in his "Cahiers" as follows:

"From Lausanne we ascended the wide Rhone Valley to Martigny, a small settlement in extreme poverty. At this point the Rhone River receives the Dranse and we entered the Dranse Valley which in a series of ascents and descents leads up to the mountain pass. We finally halted at St. Pierre, a small community on the foot of the mountain. Even though the houses of this village were small and poorly constructed, the spacious barns provided sufficient room for us to sleep in and attend to our guns and equipment. Napoleon himself was present as all cannons were taken apart in preparation for the transport over the mountain. The tubes of the three cannons

31

belonging to our artillery unit were placed into hollowed trunks of trees, but sledges and barrows were also employed as means of transportation. A strong, intelligent cannoneer with a detail of 40 grenadiers was put in charge of the transport. Being responsible for the safe transport of the material, he demanded strict obedience and tolerated no backtalk to his orders. No one was permitted to move when he shouted 'halt' and upon his command 'forward' everyone had to move on.

"Early the next morning we received our ration of rusk and two pairs of shoes per man and then started the ascent. Our cannoneer appointed twenty men to carry the trough containing the barrels of the three cannons, and while a number of other grenadiers shared the heavy burden of the body of the cannon, two men each were assigned to carry axletrees and wheels, and eight others bore the small arms.

"This ascent was one of the most arduous undertakings I ever engaged in. Silently, the men bore the heavy loads, obeying the short commands of 'halt' or 'forward' issued by our cannoneer. With the increasing steepness of the path the transport of the heavy guns became an extremely laborious and dangerous task. On one occasion we lost control of the heavy trough and it slid downhill rapidly. After hours of strenuous efforts we had the trough back in position and proceeded silently following the brief instructions and commands from our guiding cannoneer.

"Finally we were granted a moment of rest for the prime purpose of changing our shoes which ice and rocks had cut to shreds. 'Let's go, my horses,' said our cannoneer, and somewhat refreshed after hastily eating a bite of rusk, we continued our strenuous ascent.

"As we reached the regions of eternal snow and had just noticed with relief that our vehicle slid along with much less effort, we encountered General Chambarlhac. Arrogantly, the General ordered our cannoneer to increase the speed of our movement, whereupon the cannoneer harshly replied that the General was not in charge of this transport and that it was his, the cannoneer's responsibility. The General furiously stepped toward the cannoneer, who coldly advised that he would throw him in the abyss or use the loading stick on him if he interfered further.

"After several more hours of great strain and effort we viewed the roofs of the Hospice. When we were still four hundred paces distant

A corridor of the Hospice leading to the South entrance.

The cross of Great Saint Bernard.

from the buildings, we noticed a path in the snow and steps cut into the ice at the summit, which gave evidence of the presence of other troops who had previously arrived there. We put our guns down and after the rest of the four hundred grenadiers and officers had assembled at the pass, we entered the Chapel of the Monastery.

"The world-renouncing monks who occupy the Hospice have dedicated their lives to assist mankind and particularly those crossing the pass. Their large dogs are always ready to guide wayworn travelers away from the danger of avalanches and icy death into the care of the magnanimous monks. True to their tradition the monks provided sufficient bread, cheese and wine for all of us as we enjoyed the warmth of the fireplace in the large hall, and later generously prepared sleeping quarters in the spacious hallways for us. The good monks did everything in their power to make our stay comfortable and enjoyable and I believe that each of us in turn treated them with utmost consideration.

"Upon our departure the dogs accepted our caressing as if they had known us for a long time. We shook hands with the monks, unable to express sufficiently the admiration and gratitude we felt for these good men."

A Monastery dog that has been instrumental in many rescues.

The History of the
St. Bernard Dog

*A speech delivered by Professor Albert Heim at
a course for St. Bernard Judges in Berne, Switzerland, April 23, 1927*

"KNOWLEDGE increases our understanding of things and our sympathy for them." With this in mind, the St. Bernard Club requested me to speak to you on the history of the St. Bernard Dog.

According to Professor Studer and Dr. Sigmund, the Doggen type to which the St. Bernard belongs (large and powerfully built, large head, pendant ears, pronounced stop, short muzzle) has developed gradually from various breeds at different times and locations. Of numerous hypotheses that have been advanced concerning the origin of the St. Bernard dog, Studer supports that of tracing this breed back to the *Canis inostranzewi*; Sigmund considers the Saints as an oversized type of the *Canis familaris palustris* (a domesticated animal of the Stone Age); and C. Keller, as well as H. Kraemer, represent the theory that all Doggen types originate from Asia, particularly from the Thibet Mastiff.

37

The fact has definitely been established that Doggen did not exist in Switzerland in prehistoric times. Old Egyptian literature also contains no indication of the presence of this type of dog, even though the Egypt of that era was one of the few countries in which the scientific breeding of dogs was highly advanced. The first dogs of the Doggen type were imported there about 300 B.C. by Xerxes, the Greeks, Alexander the Great and the Phoenicians from Asia (Persia, Assyria, India, Himalaya).

A shipment consisting of 156 dogs was once imported by Alexander the Great for use in the arenas of old Rome. As these dogs allegedly originated at Molossis, Greece, they were identified as "Molosser" (Canis molossus) until approximately A.D. 200. There were two types of the Molosser which differed in many characteristics. One of them, which was used as sheep dog, was of slight build and light color, with a somewhat long head and easy movements. The other, heavier type, was used as protection dog and war dog. Specimens of the latter type were of dark color, with broad heads, a short muzzle and generally more heavily built. The Illyrian Molosser had prick ears, the Babylonian Molosser pendant ears. Specimens of the lighter type still exist in small numbers in the mountains of Asia. The breeds traced back to the heavy type of Molosser are Mastiffs, the old Barenbeisser, and the St. Bernard.

In the beginning the two different types of Molosser were not distinctly separated and specimens showing characteristics of either type were quite common. The Romans used these dogs for driving and guarding the herds of livestock that accompanied the armies, as well as watchdogs for their garrisons and commercial establishments, which were located in isolated valleys and at mountain passes.

All available information produces the following picture: The Asiatic dogs arrived in Helvetia (Switzerland) via Rome and the Alps in two waves. The light variety of the Molosser, the sheep dog, was the first one to migrate in the last century B.C. As they spread into the Fore-Alps they soon became animals of multiple use, serving as watchdogs at farms and homes in the valleys, as well as herding dogs and watchdogs at Alpine dairy farms. Through methodical breeding they gradually developed into a distinct breed of their own, the Swiss Alpine Dog, which, after 2,000 years, is permanently established in certain areas of Switzerland. As wolves and bears no longer jeopardize the Alpine herds, less emphasis is being put on breeding sheep dogs of white or cream color.

The second migration, during the first two centuries A.D., brought the heavier type of Molosser which remained primarily in the mountains, at pass stations and in the Valleys of Aosta and Valais. These dogs spread as far as the Bernese Oberland but remained few in number as the farmers there had acquired their dogs from the previous migration. Interested in these dogs were the wealthy aristocrats and the monks. This heavy type of the Molosser became the progenitor of the St. Bernard dog.

Literature of the past centuries contains only infrequent references to the existence of these dogs as the breeding of dogs was not cultivated in former times. The Swiss Alpine dogs, however, appear in some of the paintings by old Italian masters from 1550 to 1750. They apparently existed in the areas of Berne, Freiburg, Waadt, Unterwalden, Lucerne, St. Gallen and Appenzell.

No pictures of the St. Bernard dog are available until he appears in a painting by an unknown artist in 1695. The painting, which is now at the Hospice, pictures two dogs with typically exaggerated "Hospice" heads. They are both well built, however, one of them certainly has no double dewclaws. Their tails are quite long. A later painting, by Sir E. Landseer in 1815, shows Lion, a male imported in England from the Hospice. Lion was a very large dog of tawny color, with a sound head and no dewclaws on his hind feet. The two dogs painted in 1695, as well as Lion, resemble good specimens which could well compete with the St. Bernards of today. They prove that the distinct type of the St. Bernard was developed at that time and has remained unchanged.

Countless are the legends concerning the origin of the St. Bernard dog. One of them traces the St. Bernard back as an offspring of a dog which accidentally appeared at the Hospice. However, only one mating, or even several matings of the same type, do not create a new breed. It is also evident that the St. Bernard dog did not originate at the Hospice but was first known as the "Talhund" (Valley Dog) in the valleys and later taken to the Hospice. Years of inbreeding, with particular emphasis being placed on achieving qualifications necessary for the rescue work in the mountains, have produced the St. Bernard of today. However, the consequences of continual close line and inbreeding also manifested themselves in stillborn litters, bulldoggy heads and many other faults.

Père Roland Viot, Provost of the Order from 1611 to 1644, does not mention the dogs in his description of the Hospice and its duties. The first reference to the existence of trained rescue dogs at the Hospice was found in a rescue report of 1707 which mentions that "one dog was buried by an avalanche." In the course of his research work on the St. Bernard dog, Percy Manning, MA Oxford, discovered numerous old documents in British museums and Bodleian Libraries, among them a travel description by the Geneve Painter Bourrit. This description was written in 1774 and refers to the rescue work performed by the monks and their dogs as a fact that "has been known for a long time."

Apparently, the first dogs, descendants of the old Roman Molosser, were brought to the Hospice between 1660 and 1670 as watchdogs. The monks took them along on their walks in search for lost travelers and soon discovered their salient qualities of path finding and sense of direction. From then on the dogs were trained for guide and rescue work in which they have assisted the monks for the past 250 years with splendid results.

The records of the Hospice reveal that the dogs in 1787 protected the Hospice from a gang of burglars. During the years 1816 to 1818, years of severe snow storms, the dogs performed remarkable services and several dogs died in the course of their rescue work. In 1825 three monks, one traveler and three dogs were buried by an avalanche. The rescue work of the dogs has repeatedly been described and praised by travelers. The dogs leave the Hospice in groups, they search, find and report in groups, and many of them may have accomplished the same number of rescues (40) as Old Barry did. During the past 250 years a total of 2,000 persons have been rescued with the dogs' assistance.

It has at times been assumed that German, English or Danish Bulldogs have been crossed with the St. Bernard dogs. However, this is not true. The only occasion on which the St. Bernards were crossed with another breed was in 1830 when many of the breeding stock at the Hospice were lost due to an extremely severe winter and some disease which increased the mortality rate in puppies to almost 100 percent. In 1856 the Prior, Erw. J. Deléglise, wrote Mr. Friedrich Tschudi that the Hospice dogs were again threatened with extinction and said: "The two Newfoundlands we received last winter from Stuttgart developed very nicely, particularly the male who has started his duty in the mountains very well." (Friedrich Tschudi, *Animal Life in the Alps*). The Newfoundland here

40

referred to was the old and very heavy type which was popular in England about 1800 and several years later was represented all over the Continent. Contrary to the St. Bernard, the Newfoundland had not been degenerated through inbreeding.

After 1830 the first long haired specimens of the St. Bernard appeared. It was believed that the long hair would protect the dogs better against the cold climate, however, it soon became apparent that these long haired dogs were utterly unusable for the rescue work. After wading in the deep snow, a crust of snow and ice would completely cover the dogs and make it impossible for them to advance. The monks sold or gave away the long haired dogs, the breeding of which was continued in the valleys. Their offspring included both the short and long haired variety and several of the short haired dogs were again crossed with the dogs at the Hospice.

The breed had definitely gained, as far as strength, intelligence and character were concerned, by the temporary crossing with Newfoundlands, and after several generations the pure St. Bernard type was restored. The only indication which remained of the crossing is the long haired dog which began to exist in 1830.

The name of the breed is not old. The British named the dogs of the Hospice "Holy Dogs," "Alpine Mastiffs," "St. Bernard Mastiffs," also "Cloister Dogs," "Mountain Dogs," and "Hospice Dogs." The German canine experts suggested the name "Alpine Dogs" which, of course, would have invited the bastardizing and degeneration of the breed. In the Canton of Berne they were called the "Barryhund"; Old Barry's glory was still remembered. In 1823 Daniel Wilsen speaks of the "so-called St. Bernard Dogs," and in 1865 the name "Bernhardiner" or "St. Bernard Dog" was definitely applied. It caused much opposition as the name implied that all dogs were bred at the Hospice. This is not true since just as many or more dogs were bred in the valleys and only a few dogs had been sent to the Hospice and spread from there. The name was later interpreted more satisfactorily as "dogs, which are kept at the Hospice of St. Bernard." It was justifiable to name the dogs after the location of their rescue deeds through which they have gained world fame and popularity. The name was recognized in 1880. Brehm calls them scientifically, *Canis familaris extrarius St. Bernardi*; Fitz, *Canis extrarius alpinus*; Walther, *Molossus Monti St. Bernardi*.

The St. Bernard's qualifications that make him indispensable for

Gita-Oenz, longhaired bitch, owned by the v. Lotten Kennels of Mr. Otto Steiner of Switzerland. Gita was considered an outstanding type in her native country.

the rescue work are the never failing sense of direction and the ability to scent (in clear weather they scent a human more than 800 feet, and against the wind they scent for several miles. They are able to scent people buried 5 to 7 ft. deep in snow). The dogs also feel in advance the approach of a snow storm. About 20 to 40 minutes before the storm they become restless and want to go outside. The dogs further have the amazing ability of sensing the closeness of falling avalanches and have frequently proved this by detouring from the path which only minutes later was covered by an avalanche. Remarkable is the dogs' ability of endurance. They often remain outside for hours in temperatures 10 to 20° below and even violent snow storms do not seem to affect them.

The training of the dogs does not include punishment and orders; it is a mere matter of giving instructions; and no obedience training, as is necessary for police dogs, is involved. The dogs soon sense when they are doing right and have confidence in their masters. They follow the example of those dogs that work well and seem to desire to share their joy of success.

Remarkable is the intelligence of these dogs in their way of cooperating. If several dogs find a lost traveler in the snow they try to get him in upright position. If this is not possible, two dogs lie down on each side of him to keep him warm while others return to the Hospice and summon help. As soon as the rescue party arrives, all of the dogs remain in the background so as not to interfere with the monks' work. As soon as the victim is placed on the stretcher, the dogs lead the way back to the Hospice. No orders need to be given the dogs.

It has been observed that the offspring of good rescue dogs need little training for their work. They learn much faster than those which stem from untrained parents. The ability for rescue work seems to be hereditary and can be intensified by inbreeding. Dogs which have never received any training, but whose parents were good rescue dogs have frequently performed the services of a rescue dog in situations of danger.

St. Bernard Breeders in
Switzerland 1873 to 1904

D R. KUENZLI of St. Gallen was one of Switzerland's greatest St. Bernard breeders. Through his friendship with Dr. Kuenzli, Mr. Richard Strebel, renowned German dog writer, became acquainted with this fine breed of dogs. Over a period of years he made visits at St. Gallen which usually lasted several weeks and provided an opportunity for Mr. Strebel to become familiar with Dr. Kuenzli's kennel and his breeding aims. Dr. Kuenzli, despite all discouragements, worked ambitiously toward his goal of breeding better St. Bernards—dogs with a good gait, and a perfect build; or, as he used to say, "They must stand like horses." He was trying with steady perseverance to create a new, more modern type of the Hospice dog.

As a breeder he favored his Young Barry and expected much of him. He also owned a male, Tell, a short-coated dog, that, unfortunately in his old age, was suffering from facial atrophy. Besides these two studs Dr. Kuenzli occasionally used some stock of the old Hospice dog. It seemed, however, that the producing ability of Tell and Young Barry was not too good, as was usual with these two studs;

44

only after three generations were satisfactory results noticeable. It was his aim to breed a large dog that combined a well balanced body with the desired height. Dogs of this type were owned by breeders Egger and Schumacher. He also tried matings with the Ivo strain but he did not achieve satisfactory results.

While Young Barry's offspring developed slowly, those sired by Tell showed much beauty at an early age. The Barry strain was distinguished by a shape that seemed to be pressed together at the sides. These dogs also showed extensive black markings which gave them a somewhat dark appearance. They had wide chests and well proportioned flanks. Outstanding dogs of the Young Barry strain were Orsino, Jenatsch I and II, Olaf, Garibaldi; outstanding females were the excellent Hero v. Hirslanden and Silva-Mehlem.

Tell's progeny showed a beautiful expression and lovely colors. They had broad bodies and their coat, especially on the hindquarters, had a tendency to curl. They carried their tails high. There are Kondor (doubtless the best one), Kean I and II, Grossglockner, Young Tell, and Willy Wood, that deserve mentioning as Tell's offspring. Ilse was one of the best brood bitches produced by Tell. Bello and Bella, two of Dr. Kuenzli's dogs, won first prizes at the Basel Dog Show in 1884.

Many difficulties and sad experiences were encountered during the latter years of Dr. Kuenzli's work. His stock of approximately 70 to 80 St. Bernards, which he boarded out at neighboring farms, had been greatly reduced as some of his best dogs had been poisoned. This fact caused him almost to discontinue his work, but nevertheless, he remains one of the most outstanding breeders in the history of the St. Bernard and today receives the recognition he so duly deserves.

During the same period (1873-1904) there was another great breeder in Switzerland, Major Bloesch, at Biel, who bred for a new type of St. Bernards with imported English stock. He succeeded in improving the head in size as well as in expression. This point had been neglected by the English breeders. Young Marquis, Marquis I, and Hektor II v. Biel, were some of his best dogs. Marquis I, however, lacked in cheeks, a fact by which his English ancestry could be determined. The two other dogs showed the Swiss influence. Other outstanding dogs of his kennel were Lady Bloesch, Hektor I and Hektor II, Juno, Irma, Apollo, Herkules, Nero and Jung Bob of

W. Ernst and W. Staehli, officials of the Highland woodcarvers craft union in Brienz, Switzerland, place the date of this carving at somewhere between 1850 and 1890, judging from the carving style. They say there were several carvers doing "St. Bernhard" dogs during that time, among more than two thousand carvers working in Brienz. The number is now about four hundred.

This family of Saints is depicted in a single block of wood, 36 inches long, 18 wide, and 13 high. The figures are carved in full round, a task which must have required many hundreds of hours. All anatomical details are accurate, therefore it is assumed that the artist worked accurately to scale. By present-day standards, the mother is small in relation to the size of her pups. Muzzle shape would seem to be earlier than the 1894 painting shown on page 56, but the puppies' body shape and leg action does not seem to have changed much in a century.

The carving, still in excellent preservation, was rescued from the attic of a curio shop by Saint fancier Charles Sorenson, of Hull, Mass.

46

Biel. Several of them were sold in foreign countries for remarkable prices.

Of considerable influence in the background of many good St. Bernards was Ivo. He resulted from a mating of Leon, owned jointly by Grossrat Siegmund and Mr. Bauer, to Belline, owned by Mr. Duer at Burgdorf. Little is known of Leon's ancestors but apparently there is some Mastiff blood in his background. Ivo was a large dog with excellent colors, and a well wrinkled dark head gave him a good expression. His muzzle was well shaped without hanging jaws. His hindquarters were high and well built. Mated to his mother, Belline (later Champion "Sans Peur"), he produced the male Hektor v. Basel (later called Krupp's Hektor). This dog was sold in Germany, and even though he was not too frequently used as a stud, he had considerable influence on St. Bernards in Germany. Many offspring resulted from breedings to Ivo and it is impossible to mention all of them. Interesting is the fact that Ivo's brother, Rasco I, and his sisters, Flora and Lola Altels, developed into outstanding dogs. Flora won her championship in America.

Interested in breeding a better type of the old Hospice dog were Mrs. Deichman, wife of a Geheimrat at Cologne and later at Vaduz, Liechtenstein; Mr. Steiner at Arth; Mr. Bubat at Hirslanden; Mr. Neumaier at Zuerich; and Mr. Kohler-Grueter at Basel. Mrs. Deichman owned Lola II and later obtained the stud Pluto directly from the Hospice. Matings of these two resulted in many a good St. Bernard. Later her kennel was sold to Mr. Bubat. In 1904 it was owned by Mr. Goerin-Gerber at Hirslanden.

Good dogs of the Hospice type that were outstanding at their time were bred by Mr. Carl Steiner at Arth. From his kennel Pluto v. Arth, Young Pluto v. Arth, Bergman v. Arth, and Berry v. Arth (later Viktor Plavia) have been top dogs.

Another breeder who deserves much credit for improving the Hospice dog was Mr. Neumaier of Zuerich. In 1877 he owned Flora, a female 31 to 32 inches high. The eighties seemed to be particularly favorable years for this breeder. Mars, a male, was born in 1889; and later in the same year he obtained Hektor from Mr. Bubat's kennel. Through Hektor, Mr. Neumaier's kennel received its first Hospice stock as Hektor's ancestors were Pluto and Juno Deichman. Also in 1889 he obtained from the monastery, Jupiter and Bellona. Jupiter was an excellent sire and among his progeny we find the well known

DAUER

The three Saints shown here were all noted winners during the late twenties. They are (l. to r.) Xaba v. Taubertal (Ch. Kavalier v. Grossglockner ex Ch. Leda v. Taubertal), Ch. Leda v. Taubertal (Ch. Bernd v. Mitterfels ex Franzi v. Taubertal), Ch. Xenos v. Taubertal (Ch. Kavalier v. Grossglockner ex Ch. Leda v. Taubertal). All were bred by Hans Meyer who also owns Zaba and Leda. Xenos is owned by Ludwig Kasten.

48

Jupiter von Solothurn and Pluto Jupiter. Mr. Neumaier, however, soon realized that too much Hospice blood produced high and straight hindquarters as well as excessive white markings and uneven markings on the head (half-sided). By using Barry Fischertal he was able to outbreed these faults and then bred good dogs like Mars III and Hektor III.

Mr. Kohler-Grueter at Basel was another breeder who considered the monastery dogs the best type of St. Bernards. He tried to continue breeding in that line, and Rhyn and Barry v. Gundeldingen are to be mentioned as typical of his kennel.

St. Bernards in Switzerland into the 1970's

JUDGING by its dog shows, kennels and dog publications, Switzerland is one of the most dog-friendly nations. Swiss breeders refer to the strict kennel system, which is operated in many other countries on principles similar to that of a zoo, as "dogs' concentration camps." Swiss dog shows are always well organized and even though their preference is the homebred dog, many foreign entries are accepted at the shows. Unfortunately, Swiss dog breeding, particularly of the larger breeds, has not remained untouched by the war. However, with initiative and optimism Swiss breeders quickly overcame the difficulties of that time.

While the activities of some St. Bernard Clubs in Switzerland are known to be somewhat limited, individual breeders industriously and seriously follow their breeding programs. One of the most popular St. Bernard kennels, Von Lotten, was founded in 1925 and is owned by Mr. Otto Steiner at Muhen, Aargau. Medusa v.d. Birch, a long haired female, was purchased at the age of six weeks by Mr.

Steiner. No information on her background or breeder could be obtained. She proved to be an international success in her first year and when bred passed on her excellent qualities to her progeny. It was Mr. Steiner's policy to eliminate inferior puppies at birth and thus he was able to follow his aim of raising well balanced, strong bodied dogs, that developed a good gait, had well formed heads, a noble expression and good colors. Meta von Lotten combined all these excellent qualities and was considered the ideal St. Bernard. Besides her faultless appearance she was a good watch dog and had a most faithful disposition. At international dog shows at Den Haag, Freiburg im Breisgau, Strassburg, Muehlhausen, Zuerich, Bern and Basel, she won first prizes, and at Frankfurt-am-Main she received the title "World Champion." Her breeder, Mr. Steiner, was honored with the title of "World Champion Breeder." Meta's offspring were sold in Germany, Netherlands, America, Italy, France, North Africa, etc., and, like their famous mother, won many an international first prize. Jupiter, a Meta son, was entered at the Chicago World Dog Show.

Another proven brood bitch at the Lotten Kennels was Gita von Oenz, a daughter of Ch. Erga-Oenz, 94631 (mother of the smooth coated Ch. Figaro-Oenz and the American Ch. Gero-Oenz). Gita's mother, Erga-Oenz, was a powerfully built female with strong bones, a deep chest, a good body, excellent angulation and a kind expression. Gita inherited all of her mother's good qualities and was credited with several wins at international shows. The fact that she had a slightly arched back and was somewhat lacking in height, did not harm her excellent reputation as a brood bitch and she was considered a most valuable asset to the Lotten Kennels.

Famous among the Swiss St. Bernard Kennels is Zwing-Uri, owned by Mr. Charles Sigrist at Flüelen. Conveniently located to trains from all directions and at one of Switzerland's most romantic spots, the Lake of Lucerne, the kennel attracts many tourists. During all the years of its existence Zwing-Uri has produced a number of good dogs, many of which were exported to England and the U.S.A., as well as to Netherlands, Belgium, Italy and France. Horsa v. Zwing-Uri was sold in America where in the course of winning his championship he won a "Best of Breed" over 16 competitors, and a "Best of the Working Group." One of the best dogs owned by Zwing-Uri was

Olif, by Nero v. Zwing-Uri, out of Alma v. Zwing-Uri. Olif spent three months in France where he participated in the film, "Barry." In order to inject some new blood into his stock, Mr. Sigrist imported two St. Bernards from Germany.

Besides its fine dogs we believe that the unique setting of the kennels deserves mentioning. The kennel buildings resemble the typical Swiss frame structures and are decorated with the Coat of Arms of the Uri Canton. The buildings are located atop a rose-covered cliff, and the most amusing event of each day takes place when the serious-faced puppies climb up the steps to their houses at night. The tree-shaded kennel grounds with a small body of water provide an ideal place for the dogs.

The President of all the dog clubs in Switzerland reports that in 1951 the Saint Bernard Club in Switzerland had 115 members and that each year approximately two hundred puppies are registered. The smooth coated variety outnumbers the long haired and enjoys greater popularity.

Author's note:

During the years since this chapter was written, a cordial relationship through Saint Bernards has grown between Switzerland and the North American continent. With the latter offering wide interest and wide markets, and the former offering excellent examples of the breed, it is not surprising that a mutually profitable exchange of interest now exists.

Space does not permit a listing of the many fine dogs brought from Switzerland in recent years. Most recent imports to North America have been through the offices of Eduard Rodel, Ottenbach, Zurich, Switzerland, who operates the Sauliamt Kennels, and also acts as a bi-continental agent between the many active breeders in Switzerland and the many interested importers in North America.

The Swiss Saint and the American Saint have become very much alike. American families who acquire Saints from Switzerland find no difficulty in recognizing the appearance and habits of their imports. They discover only one major problem; that the new members of their families must be taught to understand English.

The Swiss government is interested in maintaining the excellence of Saint Bernards, as a source of national pride. Much of this work

INTERNATIONAL CHAMPION (SIEGER)
ANTON VON HOFLI

Born April 2, 1960
(S.H.S.B. 97801)
Breeder: Paul Adam, Bannwart, Oberdorf/80

Parents	G. Parents	G.G. Parents
(Sire) Bruno v. Leberberg (SHSB 68965)	Tyras v. Hanialthaus (SHSB 41462)	Caro v. Neubad Irma v. d. Lueg
	Berna v. Bellmund (SHSB 47341)	Caro v. Neubad Erla v. Schmiederain
(Dam) Cita v. Rigihang (SHSB 79738)	Pluto v. Neu-Habsburg (SHSB 46274)	Neron v. Neu-Habsburg Alma v. Morgenholz
	Asta v. Schwandenblick (SHSB 41333)	Danto v. Zwing-Uri Hulda v. Schwandenblick

53

is being done at the Monastery, with the help of the Breeders Association, whose secretary is Hans Zimmerli, of Langenthal, Switzerland. Mr. Zimmerli, one of the fancy's most respected breeders, has sent many fine Saints to North America.

St. Bernards in Germany

With research by Gerda Umlauff

GERMAN breeders had been interested in this breed several decades before the Special Club for St. Bernards was founded at Munich in 1891. More than seventy years ago these dogs were frequently referred to as "Alpenhunde." A dog magazine published in 1882 tells of considerable difficulties that were encountered by breeders at that time, among them the impossibility of tracing the ancestry of stud dogs, the lack of sufficient funds to carry on good breeding programs, and the spiteful way in which St. Bernard breeders were referred to as "Specialty Breeders" who used inferior and inbred material which they sold as St. Bernards for the sake of financial gain.

Soon, however, even those in strong opposition recognized the excellent qualities of the St. Bernard as a companion and watchdog. He was considered to be particularly useful as a companion dog to theologians on their lone walks and, because of his pleasant temperament, seemed much better qualified for this type of work than the Great Dane.

This oil painting, done in 1894, hangs in the living room of the Donald Dube home. It would seem to demonstrate that as far as the better Saint Bernards are concerned, there has not been too much change since that time. A present-day judge might say only that this dog's muzzle was a little narrow and his ears set a little too high.

Instrumental in the inauguration of the St. Bernard in Germany were three breeders: Dr. Caster of Winkle/Rheingau (also a breeder of Great Danes); Prince Albrecht of Solms and Braunfels-an-der-Lahn; and the retired Premier Lieutenant Fink of Berlin. Even though the number of dogs at that time owned by these three breeders did not exceed twelve, they deserve much credit for the promotion of the breed in Germany.

Prince Albrecht's Wolfsmuehle Kennel was one of the largest on the continent. His first import was Courage, an almost faultless male, who was later used as the model in setting up the standard for his breed in Germany. He placed first at the 1878 Berlin Show as well as in four other shows held in the Netherlands and England in 1880. Well beyond his prime he was awarded another prize at a Hannover show a few years later. A truly great show dog, his stud career seemed somewhat limited. He is known to have been bred to only a few bitches and his get was of poor quality. No records are available of his ancestors. Courage stood 35½ inches high and weighed 140 pounds; his forehead measured 28.8 inches. He was of the smooth variety and slightly feathered only on legs and neck. Contrary to the much preferred white markings on a dark basic color, Courage was of a grayish-white color and showed yellow markings.

Bred and owned by the Prince of Solms were also the males Gessler, Courage II (a Courage son out of Hedwig), and Courage III (a Courage II son out of Alp), and the females Bernina II and Hospiz, while the females Alp and Berna II had been imported from Switzerland. Exemplifying the law of alternate inheritance Courage III, at the age of 15 months, showed a strong resemblance to his famous grandsire, Courage. Even though he lacked Courage's height, he was a powerfully built dog of excellent appearance. Matings of Berna II to Courage II resulted in remarkably good offspring. There were two litters in which the puppies resembled each other almost identically, all of them having equally good markings and perfect colors, broad, expressive heads, and well developed, powerful bodies. At a Kleve Show, the Kennel Club of Aarburg showed two litters of Bernina (a litter sister to Berna II) by a stud of the Wolfsmuehle Kennels. (The stud's name is not mentioned here and it is known only that the same dog was later sold to Switzerland.) Several of the Wolfsmuehle dogs were sold in Switzerland, as good stud dogs had become scarce there.

57

GONNY V.D. EILSHORST
16370.

ZENO VOM GROSSGLOCKNER 12767,
Longhaired German male.

58

While English breeders were able to exhibit some good St. Bernards at that time, Germany showed only specimens of the long haired variety. The smooth coated type was hardly represented. Among the questions pertaining to the standard of the St. Bernard was the one as to whether a reddish-brown nose was acceptable. Mr. Hartenstein, a well-known breeder, imported a female from Interlaken, Switzerland, and bred her to two different studs. Each of the two litters showed the reddish-brown coloring of the nose and even though the puppies were good in many other points, Mr. Hartenstein decided to eliminate them. (The color of the nose was at that time not mentioned in the standard but received recognition at a later time.)

According to Dr. Caster, none of the large breeds at that time were in as much a state of decline as was the St. Bernard. In his opinion there was not one St. Bernard in Germany that came up to the standard, and he did not expect the available mediocre dogs to be good producers. Referring to British St. Bernards, he stressed the large number of beautiful dogs entered in the shows and the fact that British breeders had for some time been using only the very best stock, for which they paid enormous prices. It was Dr. Caster's suggestion that a Club or several interested fanciers join in the purchase of an outstanding female which was to be bred to one of the best studs in England and the resulting offspring then would constitute a fine breeding stock for Germany. Dr. Caster based his advice to import British St. Bernards on the fact that many of the long haired St. Bernards imported from Switzerland were beautiful in appearance but seldom the result of good breeding and in most cases of poorest heredity.

At the 1882 Hannover All Breed Dog Show, 36 dogs were entered as long haired St. Bernards—"Alpenhunde." In addition to these, several Newfoundlands of untraceable ancestry were put in the same group. Of these approximately 40 dogs, nine males and three females received prizes. However, only six of them were considered purebred St. Bernards. The others resembled the Alpenhunde or some equally large breed. The presentation of prizes to these dogs met with considerable astonishment and disapproval on the part of the breeders and promoters of the purebred St. Bernard. The large, long haired dogs were known as "Leonbergers" and their ancestry could easily be traced to several different large half-breeds. Some of these dogs, which were raised chiefly in Wuerttemberg, had impressive, powerful bodies, but it was quite obvious that there had been no St. Bernards in their background. For several years consistent efforts had been made to eliminate this type of dog, and we can understand the anger and disappointment of the serious breeders when these mongrels received prizes at a show and were classed as St. Bernards. Foul play was suspected, but the judge, an Englishman, insisted that he was in no way involved in any disreputable actions.

First Prize at the Hannover Show was awarded to Cadwallader, a large male of excellent color and strong bone. Particularly impressive were his mighty head and the well proportioned muzzle, but also his fine reddish color and the white markings. Gessler, a male owned by the Prince of Solms, placed second. He showed gray markings on a white basic color and had a beautiful large head and a noble expression.

Two more Wolfsmuehle dogs were entered in the show but they did not place. They showed the results of excellent grooming, but incorrect carriage of their tails disqualified them. Courage III was entered but was faulted on account of his narrow forehead, his somewhat pointed nose and lack of stop. His father, Courage II, also did not place at this show. This seemed somewhat unusual, as Courage II was indeed a good dog; and even though his head lacked broadness, it was much better than that of his son Courage III.

Showgoers were most favorably impressed by the smooth coated St. Bernards for these seemed to be well behaved dogs of a kind disposition. Because of these qualities they desired to help the St. Bernard gain more popularity, and it was felt that they soon would constitute a serious competition for the Great Dane.

The average of the St. Bernards shown at Hannover in 1882 left much to be desired, particularly as far as gait and hindquarters were concerned. Careful selection of breeding material and the necessity of physical exercise for young dogs were stressed in an effort to improve the breed. It was known that at the same time the average Swiss St. Bernard was of much better quality.

During the years following the Hannover Show, more breeders became interested in St. Bernards and started breeding programs with good stock. They willingly paid high stud fees for the best foreign studs and also invested considerable money in importations.

ALTONA'S ALF 13923

CH. GISA V. LUDWIGSTEIN 16952.

Gisa received champion title and "excellent" first prize at Munich in 1948, at Mannheim in October 1948, "excellent" first prize and Mannheim, May 1949, "excellent" first prize.

61

A headstudy and full-body portrait of Lutjer v. Hemphorn. These photographs were taken about 1936.

Besides the Prince of Solms, who later imported the male Barry Braunfels from Switzerland and several other St. Bernards from England, Mr. Hartenstein of Plauen enlarged his kennel through imports. In 1884 in the Rhone Valley he purchased Rocher, an excellent stud; and later he imported from Switzerland Finette II, Fels, Phaedra, Prinz v. Burgdorf, Torone, Tamina, Victor Plavia, Jungfrau, and Grossglockner. Prinz v. Burgdorf was considered the most outstanding of all these importations. Unfortunately, only a few years later the Hartenstein Kennel ceased to exist, as did also the Wolfsmuehle Kennel upon the death of Prince of Solms in 1901.

Other breeders carried on the work. Of them we know Dr. Calaminus of Langendiebach, Mr. Probst and Mr. Pingerra, both of Munich. Mr. Pingerra imported from Switzerland Rawyl v. Atburg (SHSB 16), Watzmann, Pilatus, Beresina, Belisar (16), Queen (287) and several others. However, he seemed to have little success in raising good dogs. As St. Bernards were much in demand at that time, he apparently tried to breed for quantity rather than quality and started crossing St. Bernard stock with long haired mongrels. This was a grave and unforgivable mistake. While the St. Bernard ancestry was still distinguishable in the first few litters, the mongrel blood soon predominated. Fortunately, the St. Bernard Club came into existence at that time and made the continuation of this type of breeding impossible.

One of the oldest and most successful St. Bernard breeders was Mr. G. Schmidtbauer of Munich, who imported from Switzerland Herakles (31), Saentis, Barry (49), a half brother to Krupp's Hektor (29), Berna, Troja (146), Priest (218), Meta II (615), and Barry Frauenfeld (213), and with these dogs founded his famous kennel, Munichia. Isis, a female by Krupp's Hektor out of Queen, and Troja, were the kennel's best brood bitches. Isis was later sold to Dr. Zeppenfeld and mated to Young Meder. While Isis was a typical descendant of the Ivo strain, Young Meder was the result of a most fortunate mixture of English and Swiss blood. The best offspring produced by Isis and Young Meder was Othello. For a long time the Munichia kennel held the first place among the St. Bernard breeders in Germany. Its dogs, the famous Ch. of Munichia Lord (842), Ch. Munichia Pierette (1593), Munichia Ivo (1302), Munichia Rival (2266), Munichia Sparta (279), have laid the foundation for the St. Bernard breeding in Germany and are found in nearly all of today's German pedigrees.

Dr. Toelle, at Muehlheim/Baden, was another German breeder of good St. Bernards. He owned Peter v. Muehlheim, Gesserl, Tell-Pirna and Bello-Kalk, all belonging to the same litter out of Turka by Grossglockner. One of Dr. Toelle's famous dogs, the smooth coated Bergmann, died of injuries received in a dog fight with Peter v. Muehlheim.

Other well known breeders of that time were the painter R. F. Curry of Munich; Bubat of Mehlem; Guerteler of Munich; Kohn of Ravensburg and later of Augsburg; Boppel of Canstatt, and Max Naether of Munich. Famous dogs like Wodans Rasko (1409), Wodans Barry (1091)—one of the greatest St. Bernards that ever lived—Wodan v. Schwabing (701), Wodans Saturn (1969), Wodans Stella (2982), Wodans Heidi (3019), came from the Wodans Kennels owned by Mr. Naether. All of these fine dogs resulted from well planned matings between the Hospiz, Deppeler, Munichia and Herkules v. Bern strains.

Not to be forgotten as one of the popular kennels at that time is the Urach Kennel, owned by Mr. Kempel. It seems that incorrect pedigrees interfered very unfavorably with Mr. Kempel's carefully planned breeding program, and he had to overcome many discouraging experiences before he established his kennel's bloodline. He was particularly interested in obtaining dogs with a good disposition, a goal which he finally achieved. Some of his best dogs were Athos, Tell, Ch. Barry Urach, and the females Flora v. Basel, her daughter Gemma, Blanka Urach (dam of Barry Urach) and Norma Urach (a Rosette daughter), which later produced the famous champions Wotan v. Elberfeld and Ada v. Plankstadt. After twenty years of breeding, Mr. Kempel, in an effort to revive the old Hospice strain, purchased the male Jupiter (Sire: Tuerk, Dam: Liaune) from the Hospice.

Of the ladies interested in breeding St. Bernards we know Mrs. Johanna Nickau, wife of a brewery owner; Mrs. Deichmann of Mehlem; the Countess Larisch of Munich; and Baroness v. Moll at Villa Lagarina in Austria. Mrs. Nickau's kennel was located at Gohlis near Leipzig and besides St. Bernards she raised some toy breeds. Other breeders of that time were the gentlemen: Bostelmann of Meckelfeld, Fehn of Erlangen, Groos of Wiesbaden, Hoffmann of Hannover, Krause of Dresden, Landfried of Obergerlachsheim, Latz of Euskirchen, Probst of Munich, Teufel of Tuttlingen, Wachendorf of Steglitz, and the Austrian breeders Schinle of Meran and Puch and Seidler of Graz.

Famous St. Bernards at the end of the 19th Century were Barry v. Goeppingen II (452), Barry Saulgau I (152), Barry Saulgau II (465) and Barry Canstatt.

At that time several breeders in Netherlands endeavored to breed good St. Bernards. We know of Mr. Steensma, Dr. Lange and Mr. P. Attema, who purchased their stock from Swiss and German kennels and produced a number of fine dogs which, in turn, at a later time, were bought by German breeders of the Rheinland.

The first *St. Bernard Stud Book* published in Germany in 1894 contained 301 registrations, 175 smooth coated and 126 long haired St. Bernards. These figures prove that the St. Bernard, hardly known in Germany a few years back, now had become the most popular of the large breeds. In fact, the St. Bernard outranked the Great Dane. Also listed in the 1894 *Stud Book* are the purpose and aims of the St. Bernard Club which primarily deal with the improvement of type, body, size, color and markings.

Many a famous kennel was founded before the close of the 19th Century, with Bavaria taking the lead over Baden, Wuerttemberg and Northern Germany. To mention a few of these kennels, there were Von Moeckern, Von Kronental, Von Dessau, Von Langenstein, Von Duesseldorf, and Von Altona. (the Altona Kennels are considered the oldest St. Bernard kennels in Germany.)

The Guetsch Kennels, owned by Mr. Mannuss at Lucerne, were founded in Switzerland at that time, and with the importation of the stud Rigi von Dessau, Mr. Mannuss intended to bring some new blood into his stock. The majority of the Swiss breeders resented this transaction, but the fact remains that the Guetsch kennels produced famous St. Bernards.

Outstanding stud dogs in Southern Germany at that time were the litter brothers Ch. Troubadour v. Duesseldorf (1397) and Barry v. Fuerth (1324).

In the minutes of the monthly meetings of the Verein der Hundefreunde (Association of Dog Lovers) reference is made to the most common faults of the St. Bernard of that time. Apparently, most of the dogs were too light in muzzle, lacked broadness of the head, carried their tails incorrectly and were generally too small and too long in body. The St. Bernard Club tried in many ways to educate its

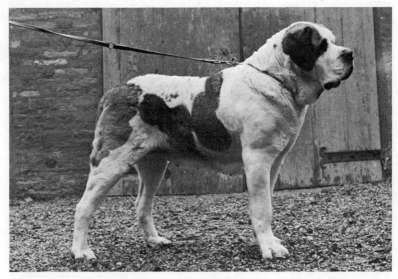

Int. Ch. (Bundesiegerin) Zenta von Bismarkturm 25356, Smooth bitch.
Sire: Alex v. Alten Berg (rough)   Breeder: Alois Schmid
Dam: Ursi von Bismarkturm (smooth)   Owner: Dr. Antonio Morsiani (Italy)

members and assist them in raising better dogs. Mr. Boppel, who in his long experience as a judge had obtained extensive knowledge of this breed, sketched and published the four different types of head that appeared most frequently around 1905.

From 1906 to 1909 some of the best St. Bernards shown were Prinz v. Stadtilm (2249), Ch. Argos v.d. Hammerburg (2269), Ch. Wola v. Stadtilm (2248), Ch. Prinz v. Goeppingen (2782), Ch. Barry v. Goeppingen (2350), Pyrrhus v. Lauben-Urach (2728), Lola v. Bernhardinerheim (2351), Ch. Thalattas Iduna (2569) and Ch. Nonne v. Fuerstenfeld (2085). German breeders deserve much credit for improving the St. Bernard in type and body. Their untiring efforts were rewarded when finally German St. Bernards had achieved the same degree of perfection as those in Switzerland. Of course, they encountered many reverses during World War I when the breeding of St. Bernards almost came to a standstill. Lack of food during the war years necessitated the elimination of a large number of dogs and only the very best specimens were kept alive. Compared to the 800 studbook entries from 1912 to 1914, the number of dogs registered from October 1914 to February 1922 seems alarmingly small. In this eight-year period only 202 litters (a total of 1,108 puppies) and 217 single dogs were registered.

All such discouraging experiences did not keep Mr. Ludwig Kasten from continuing his work toward improving the St. Bernard. Mr. Kasten, who had founded his Altona Kennels in 1897, was one of the most successful breeders in Germany and was appointed judge by the St. Bernard Club in 1909. As the size of the St. Bernard in Northern Germany after World War I left much to be desired, Mr. Kasten began his search for a large stud dog with which he intended to accomplish some improvements. After numerous efforts he finally located in Bavaria Ch. Xenos v. Taubertal (9715), by Ch. Kavalier v. Grossglockner (7741) out of Ch. Leda v. Taubertal (8040). However, at first his offers to buy the dog were refused, and only his persistent efforts and several trips to Bavaria finally made the purchase of the dog possible. Ch. Xenos' influence on St. Bernards in Northern Germany was remarkable, and he brought the breed to new heights. Many of his offspring won champion titles—to mention only Ch. Greif v.d. Helenenburg, Ch. Gretel v.d. Helenenburg, Ch. Nelson v. Falkenstein, and Ch. Dieter v. Norden who later was sold in Southern Germany. After Xenos' death, Mr. Kasten

GERT BELMONT S.H.S.B. 43383 (left) (Ch. Rasko v. d. Reppisch 11127 SHSB
29106—DORA BELMONT SHSB 32098). Bern, 1933. Breeder: G. Giavina, Bern,
Switzerland.
APOLLO ROUGANG S.H.S.B. 46431 (right) (Ch. Rasko v. d. Reppisch 11127 SHSB
29106—ADDA PARA SHSB 29055). Bern, 1933. Breeder: G. Giavina, Bern, Switzerland.

leased for two months Ch. Aegir v.d. Scheerenburg who, like Xenos, was a Ch. Kavalier v. Grossglockner son. Aegir sired the male Altona's Alf (13923), a fine dog that won many an "excellent" at the shows but unfortunately was poisoned and died at an early age. One of the fine qualities of Mr. Kasten's dogs was their kind disposition. As an example of Xenos' good disposition Mr. Kasten relates the following incident: One night he was awakened by the furious barking of Xenos. Looking outside for the cause of the disturbance, he saw his pet cat trapped. When the cat was freed, Xenos immediately took him to his doghouse and licked his little playmate's injured leg.

Another well known kennel in Northern Germany was Mr. Zillinger's Von Falkenstein, founded in 1909. His stock consisted of the imported bitch Toja Guetsch (43406), and the stud Ch. Theo's Minka v. Falkenstein (3396). Matings of these two produced a number of famous St. Bernards, among others Ch. Wanda v. Falkenstein (3582) and Ch. Kora v. Falkenstein (10493) who won her championship in 1933. After the 1935 World Dog Show at Frankfurt, a Dutch specialist, Mr. de la Rie, wrote in the *Swiss Dog Magazine* that the success of the German St. Bernards would have been much greater if the long haired dogs of Mr. Zillinger had been half a year older. He said: "These young dogs have been the greatest surprise at the show and I am convinced that Mr. Zillinger will be very successful in the future. It must have been a great honor for him that at this show, where breeders from Germany, Switzerland, Austria, France and Netherlands met, all congratulated him." Mr. Zillinger died in 1943, and at present all that is left of the Falkenstein Kennels lives in the memory of Mr. Zillinger's children who well remember the times when they rode to school in a small cart which was drawn by one of the St. Bernards.

Founded shortly before the outbreak of World War I was the Grossglockner Kennel, owned by Mr. H. Glockner, at that time president of the German St. Bernard Club. In 1914 Mr. Glockner purchased the stud Rigi v. Hessen (4565), by Ch. Tangua v. Rheinland (31315) out of Ch. Rene v. St. Michael (3300). Rigi later won his championship. Outstanding males of the Grossglockner Kennel were Armin v. Grossglockner (5041) who later sired the famous Ch. Bernd v. Mitterfels (6031); Art v. Grossglockner (5031); Baer v. Grossglockner (5105), a Rigi son; Dunmar v. Grossglockner

(5683); Ch. Kavalier v. Grossglockner (7741); and Rasco v. Grossglockner (10310). Mr. Glockner preferred to keep not more than twelve dogs at a time at his kennel as he liked to observe them individually and remain in close contact with them. Not too many of his dogs were seen in the show ring, as his frequent assignments as judge prevented him from entering his own dogs. One of the outstanding dogs of the Grossglockner Kennel after World War I was the smooth coated Wito v. Grossglockner (12457), whelped in 1932 and sired by the famous Ch. Fritz Drei Lilien (9782), whose ancestry can be traced back to the Swiss Ch. Emir Jura (SHSB 15532), Susi v. Grossglockner (10625), Kavalier v. Grossglockner (7741) and Jutta v. Grossglockner (6989), thus carrying the strain of Ch. Bernd v. Mitterfels (6031) and Baer v. Grossglockner (5105). The long haired male Zeno v. Grossglockner (12767) was another fine stud dog. He resulted from a mating of the famous Eros Guetsch (SHSB 32205), an Emir Jura (SHSB 15532) son out of Netti Deppeler (SHSB 27623), to Ulla v. Grossglockner, a Jutta v. Grossglockner daughter. In 1934 a repeated breeding of Eros Guetsch and Ulla v. Grossglockner produced some excellent smooth haired Saints.

Other kennels which started their breeding programs before the war and continued during and after the war were Von Alsatia, Von Freudenfels, Von Asyl, Von Rheinland, Von Elberfeld, Von Crimmittschau, Von der Vorstadt, Vom Taubertal, Von den Drei Lilien, Von Eistobel, etc. Ch. Tangua v. Rheinland (3135), Ch. Castor v. Freudenfels (6653), Ch. Tasso I v. Freudenfels (5147), Ch. Rigi v. Hessen (4565), Ch. Estor v. Taubertal (5424), Ch. Bernd v. Mitterfels (6031), and Ch. Elmire v. Rheinland (3140) were some of the excellent dogs produced by these kennels. There were many admirers for these dogs, particularly from Switzerland and other foreign countries. A Swiss dog magazine admitted that the German St. Bernards exhibited at the Munich Show in 1926 were of much better quality than those available in Switzerland at the same time. Top stud dogs of the year 1923 were Samson v. Eistobel (4772), Barry Jura (5195), Arth v. Grossglockner (5032), Barry v. Memmingerberg (5926).

Northern and Southern Germany were in friendly competition with each other in raising the better dogs, and in 1925 Northern Germany took the lead with fine dogs like Argos v.d. Blattgoldstadt, Arno v. Helenenburg, Goswin v.d. Waldau and Minka v.d. Kollauburg.

70

Ch. Dieter v. Norden.

Wito v. Grossglockner.

Kavalier v. Grossglockner.

Ch. Nelson v. Falkenstein, shown in full-body
and in head study was a well-known German-
bred Saint of the forties.

These three Saints earned themselves a place of honor in the permanent history
of the breed. They are (l. to r.) Int. Ch. Emir v. Jura bred by Herr Leuenberger-
Hess, Rasko v.d. Reppisch bred by Dr. Wachter and Gert Belmont bred by
G. Giavina. All were Swiss-bred.

In 1934, the fortieth year of its existence, seventeen volumes of the *St. Bernard Stud Book* had been published. A total of 13,200 Saints had been registered up to that time and 1,124 kennel names had been granted. With a total of 313 dogs shown during 1934, St. Bernards ranked in tenth position among the popular breeds. The 1,200 St. Bernards listed in Volume 17 of the *Stud Book* consisted of 940 long haired and 260 smooth haired dogs. Breeders expressed the desire to breed more smooth coated dogs in the future.

Also listed in the *Stud Book* are 11 stud dogs that had been used on five or more occasions during a two-year period. They are:

Ch. Fritz v. Drei Lilien (9782)
Baldo v. Wiesental (9917)
Ch. Abs v. Gruenau (10406)
Falk v. Hemphorn (10670)
Iseg Margothof (11237)
Ingo v. Rigi (13052)

Arth v.d. Scherenburg (9830)
Rasko v. Grossglockner (10310)
Armin v. Ranshofen (10590)
Henze Margothof (11135)
Ch. Nero v. Uhlenhorst (12039)

Falk (10670) and Nero (12039), both of Swiss parentage, were credited with the largest number of breedings. Fritz (9782) also had some Swiss blood in his background as his sire was the famous Ch. Emir Jura. Ingo (13052) was a Swiss importation.

The breed profited greatly from a decision of the St. Bernard Club which set the minimum age for a stud dog at two years and that of a brood bitch at 20 months. Two regulations released by the St. Bernard Club at a later date contributed much to the improvement of the breed. One of them limited the use of a brood bitch to once a year and the other limited to six the number of puppies to be raised in one litter. Not more than six puppies of a litter were eligible for registration in the *Stud Book*.

Seventy-nine St. Bernards were entered at the 1935 World Dog Show at Frankfurt-am-Main. This shows a considerable increase compared with 12 entries at Hamburg in 1869, and 42 entries in 1876. The largest number of entries ever recorded was 157 in 1907 at Munich. At the Frankfurt show in 1935 the German-bred St. Bernards were of such excellent quality that only the best and fully matured Swiss dogs were able to compete against them. Sixty-one long haired and eighteen short coated dogs were entered.

The Nazis, in 1937 at the height of their success and dominating everything, tried to interfere with the breeding of St. Bernards. *Das Schwarze Korps*, a publication of the SS, attempted to convince German readers of the undesirable characteristics of the St. Bernard. They called attention to the shape of the St. Bernard's head and eyes as an indication of viciousness and at one time printed an article according to which a girl had been torn to pieces by a vicious St. Bernard that had then to be shot. The Nazis also prohibited the awarding of the titles Club Champion and International Champion (CACIB). At the beginning of World War II the Nazis planned to train St. Bernards as rescue and first aid dogs for Alpine units. The St. Bernard appealed to them for this purpose, as he combines a strong body and a good gait with the capability of endurance.

In this connection it may be mentioned that St. Bernards have been useful and reliable as seeing-eye dogs. One blind person had over a period of years owned various breeds of dogs and finally found in the St. Bernard the quiet, unexcitable, reliable dog fit for this type of duty. Another blind person, who had previously owned a German Shepherd dog, purchased an eight-months-old St. Bernard which he, with the assistance of his Shepherd, trained as a guide dog. After a short training period the St. Bernard proved that his intelligence and ability were far superior to that of the German Shepherd and he never lost his tranquillity and kindness. As a salesman, the owner of this dog travelled extensively, and this placed a difficult task on his guide dog. However, the dog adjusted himself to new surroundings amazingly fast and was able on the first visit to a new city to lead his master safely back to the railroad station upon his request.

Unfortunately, World War II did much harm to the breeding of good St. Bernards in Germany. In 1939 only 172 were registered and 224 in 1941. However, the demand for reliable companion and watch dogs continued to exist, and German breeders attempted to continue their breeding programs even though lack of food and other hardships inflicted by the war made it almost impossible. As money was practically worthless during that time, the dogs were bartered for food and other useful articles. The demand for purebred dogs did not cease to exist until June 1948 when the new German currency became effective. It was then lack of money that made the purchase of good dogs impossible.

From March 1944 to December 1946, 145 litters with a total of

INTERNATIONAL CH. (SIEGER) EMIR v. JURA
Rough-Coated Male
Born November 10, 1922
(S.H.S.B. 15,532)

Parents	G. Parents	G.G. Parents
Sire Cuno v. Jura (S.H.S.B. 10,341)	s Fleck— (Cardinaux) d Bella— (Waldvogel)	(Third generation names not available in America.)
Dam Freya v. Leberberg (S.H.S.B. 10,510)	s Rasco—Riesbach d Belline v. Leberberg	

646 puppies were registered. Forty-three of these litters consisted of at least 10 or more puppies. Baerbel v. Birkenberg (447) no doubt set the record with a litter of 20 puppies. She had previously whelped litters of 15, 18 and 17.

According to the *Stud Book*, the following numbers of litters were registered:

	Number of Litters
Name of Kennel	*of Litters*
Von Hannoverland	44
Von Bismarckturm	28
Von Lehnitzsee	27
Von Werdenfels	25
Von der Koenigsmuehle	21
Total	145

Four sires share in 90 (62 percent) of these litters with a total of 407 single registrations. They are:

	Number of Litters
Sire	*of Litters*
Ch. Dieter v. Norden (14502)	14
Omen v. Hemphorn (15375)	22
Ch. Kuno v. Sonneberg VKV 324	23*
Jochem v. Lautrach (13974)	11

---

* Bred in Czechoslovakia.

Other successful stud dogs were Cuno v. Ludwigstein (15432), Boto v. Bismarckturm (15701), Dieter v. Bismarckturm (16135), a Cuno son, Page v. Hemphorn (15814), Czar v.d. Falkenhoehe (16328), Pluto v. Sonneberg (17157), Lord v. Lautrach (15387), Kuno v. Werdenfels (16423), Drusus v. Willkamm (15319) and Guenther v. Kottmar (15369).

It was no doubt a remarkable achievement that was accomplished by the German breeders during those war years as shortages of all kinds complicated their work to a large extent. In 1945 the old name of St. Bernard Club was restored after the Nazis had changed it to "Fachschaft fuer Bernhardiner." The Club has now 500 members, and close to 2,500 Saints have been registered since 1945.

CH. BERNA v.d. LUEG-WALDECK
Rough-Coated Female
Born October 30, 1931
(S.H.S.B. 45,779—A.K.C. 767,319)

Parents	G. Parents	G.G. Parents
Sire Bayard v. Riesbach (S.H.S.B. 25,573)	s Sieger Emir v. Jura	s Cuno v. Jura d Freya v. Leberberg
	d Berna v. Schloss Blidegg	s Tristan v. Rafz d Wanda-Oenz
Dam Freya v. Bergbruennli (S.H.S.B. 35,149)	s Sieger Rasko v.d. Reppisch-Waldeck	s Sieger Emir v. Jura d Gerda— (Winzeler)
	d Berna— (Gruber)	s Bayard—Zytglogge d Dora— (Gruber)

77

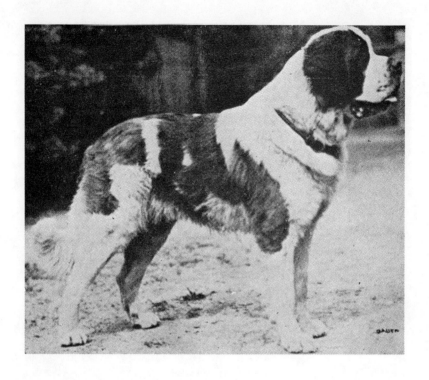

INTERNATIONAL CH. (SIEGER) RASKO
v.d. REPPISCH-WALDECK
Rough-Coated Male
Born December 12, 1927
(S.H.S.B. 29,106—A.K.C. 867,315)

Parents	G. Parents	G.G. Parents
		s Fleck— (Cardinaux)
Sire	s Cuno v. Jura	d Bella— (Waldvogel)
Sieger Emir v. Jura (S.H.S.B. 15,532)	d Freya v. Leberberg	s Rasco—Riesbach
		d Belline v. Leberberg
	s Tristan v. Rafz	s Barry—Oenz
Dam		d Freya—Neuhof
Gerda (Winzeler) (S.H.S.B. 18,322)	d Diana— (Bachmann)	s Stolz—Gutsch
		d Berna—Alt Mars

78

ULI v. BERG und NEHL posed for "breed type" in this 1932 photograph. Notice, especially, the head type and absence of freckling on this handsome specimen.

NERO v. HEMMENTHEL, a fine European specimen of the early 1930's, gives us his Saintliest expression.

79

ST. BERNARD AND HIS DOG

This beautiful stained glass window in Feltham Church, Middlesex, England,
shows St. Bernard of Menthon and one of his famous dogs.

St. Bernards in England

THE first St. Bernards, which were imported in Britain in the early part of the nineteenth century, were somewhat odd looking specimens. In 1815, Mrs. Boode of Leasowe Castle, near Birkenhead, imported a male, Lion, and a bitch (name unknown). Little else is known of Lion except the fact that he and two of his offspring so attracted the famous painter, Landseer, that he begged permission to paint them.

According to specialists, English breeders imported Swiss dogs with the intention of improving their English Mastiffs. However, they soon began to raise pure St. Bernards which, apparently, were quite a different type from the original Swiss dogs. One of the reasons for this difference in appearance was that the British preferred an almost self-colored fawn which to some extent resembled a Mastiff. The Swiss, being somewhat shrewd businessmen, imported Mastiffs and crossed them with mongrels. The resulting half-breeds were well paid for by Englishmen and so were the red and fawn colored St. Bernards which did not appeal to the Swiss breeders. The British, however, became dissatisfied with these medium-sized imported St. Bernards and started breeding their own. They bred for large dogs and aimed for the much desired red color.

This newly created type differed in size and color as well as shape of head from the Swiss dogs. They had narrow noses with little push-up and not too well defined stops; their cheeks were less pronounced and even though their heads were well wrinkled, they lacked the typical St. Bernard expression. This fact is attributed to possible crossings with Bloodhounds. In more recent years, both Swiss and English breeders prefer the Swiss type and aim to breed large-sized dogs with good colors.

Mr. Albert Smith is said to have owned some Hospice dogs, but no pedigrees are available to support this statement. Imports of significance were Mr. Macdona's Tell (later Monarque) and Mr. Stone's Barry, who later appears in many of the best English bloodlines, among them that of Plinlimmon. Studs of equal ability were Mr. Charles Isham's Leo, once owned by Mr. Egger, and Mr. Gresham's Abbess. Some of the first British breeders were Mr. J. C. Macdona, Mr. Murchinson, Mr. Gresham and Rev. Arthur Carter. Outstanding St. Bernards, which were also well known on the continent, were Plinlimmon, Bayard and Sir Bedivere.

The appellation "St. Bernard" was adopted in 1862 when some of the imported dogs were exhibited at a Birmingham show. Up to that time they had been identified as "Alpine Mastiffs" or "Alpine Spaniels." (Major Hamilton Smith, 1827.) In the middle of the last century the size and beauty of the St. Bernard captured the fancy of many an exhibitor and within twenty years this breed claimed first place in popularity. Together with Collies they were responsible for inaugurating an era of high prices. According to a newspaper notice in 1880, a Sheffield dog, Rector, had been sold in America for £300 which, at that time, was a considerable amount of money. However, this amount was completely dwarfed a few years later when Sir Bedivere was purchased by two Americans for £1,300. Sir Bedivere weighed well over 200 pounds and measured 33½ inches at the shoulder.

Further study of the St. Bernard history in England reveals that at the 1891 Charles Cruft Show (the first one open to all breeds) 34 competitors were entered in the Novice Class, 23 in Open Dogs, and 20 in Open Bitches. Soon after this show, however, St. Bernards

CH. PELDATOR MARCUS, owned and bred in the 1960's by Mrs. R. L. Walker, then president of the United St. Bernard Club of England. The English have been fond of large Saints. Marcus, photographed at three years, stands over 36 inches at the shoulder and weighs 230 pounds. Many of his offspring have been brought to the United States.

began to deteriorate in quality as well as in number. Only the Bowdon Kennels, owned by Messrs. Inman and Walmsley, continued their breeding program. Referring to them, popular dog writer A. Smith is quoted as saying, "It is believed that these breeders introduced a Mastiff cross; but whatever they did, there is no doubt that they bred St. Bernards with remarkable consistency, and their dogs were noted for their soundness as well as type. It was a serious blow when their kennels were broken up, and the breed never recovered." Mr. Smith also stated that in more recent years Mrs. Staines of Abbots Pass Kennels at Leigh, near Reigate, established a kennel which was considered a model of its kind. The kennel buildings were among the best in the country and her dogs were noted for size and quality. Mrs. Staines imported several dogs from Switzerland which were expected to be of considerable influence on succeeding generations. Dogs of Mrs. Staines' kennel soon became a familiar sight at the shows and were distinguished by their size and nobility of expression.

The official standard for the St. Bernard in Great Britain is as follows:

The HEAD should be large and massive, the circumference of the skull being rather more than double the length of the head from nose to occiput. The muzzle is short, full in front of the eye and square at the nose end. The cheeks are flat and there is great depth from eye to lower jaw. The lips are deep, but not too pendulous. The stop is somewhat abrupt and well defined. The skull is broad, slightly rounded at the top and has a somewhat prominent brow. The whole effect should be to give an expression betokening benevolence, dignity and intelligence. The ears are of medium size, lying close to the cheeks and not too heavily feathered. The eyes are rather small, deep set and dark in color. They should not be too close together and the lower eyelid droops so as to show a fair amount of haw.

The CHEST is wide and deep, the back broad and straight, the ribs well rounded, the loin wide and very muscular.

The FORELEGS should be perfectly straight, strong of bone and good of length; the HINDLEGS heavy in bone with hocks well bent and thighs muscular.

As for SIZE, the taller the better, provided symmetry is maintained. They should have great substance and the general outline should suggest power and capability of endurance.

In the long haired variety the COAT should be dense and flat, rather full around the neck, thighs well feathered.

COLORS may be orange, mahogany brindle, red brindle, or white with patches on body of either of the above colors. Importance is attached to the manner in which the markings are distributed.

Early American Breeders

THE first St. Bernard to be registered in the National American Kennel Club, whose stud books were later taken over by the American Kennel Club, was CHIEF, a smooth coated male owned by Mr. A. V. de Goicowria, New York City; Breeder, Mr. J. P. Haines, Toms River, New Jersey; whelped May 12, 1879; orange, tawny and white; by Harold, out of Judy; Harold by Sultan III, out of Dido II; Judy by Chamounix, out of Alphe.

In this same stud book the rough coated dog, Hermit, the rough coated bitch, Nun and the smooth coated bitches, Alma, Brunhild and Chartreuse, all owned by Miss Anna H. Whitney, Lancaster, Massachusetts, were registered.

Hector seems to be a popular name during the early years of the stud book. Volumes III, IV and V of the stud book were issued quarterly and in the last quarter of Volume V, Hector I, 11851 appears, owned by James Dunne, of Brooklyn, New York; breeder, Colonel White, Long Branch, New Jersey; whelped April 26, 1887; tawny and white, black facings; by Neptune out of Nellie. From then on we have a series of "Hectors" until we reach Champion Hector, a smooth coated dog, whelped February 20, 1894, A.K.C. 4425. This dog played a prominent part in the bloodlines of the early St. Bernards. He was bred by Henry Schumacher, Berne, Switzerland, and imported by Mr. K. E. Hopf of the Hospice Kennels, of Arlington, New Jersey. His height at the shoulders was 30½ inches.

In criticism, Mason states that the head was well formed but would be still better if wider; muzzle also of good formation and could only be improved by having more width; ears correct in size, shape, position and carriage; eyes well set and exactly the right color; stop excellent; expression most pleasing indicative of dignity, courage and good nature combined; neck muscular and of ample length; shoulders well placed; chest truly formed in every direction; loin firm and nicely arched; hindquarters well set and supported by rare good legs and feet; hocks clean, strong and well bent; elbows not very well placed; legs straight and strong; feet of the very best kind; coat could not be better; his stud fee was $100.

Writing in the *American Dog Book*, published in 1891, Mr. F. E. Lamb tells us, and we quote: "The development of St. Bernard interests in America has been remarkably rapid during the past ten years, and is illustrative of that enterprising spirit and that marked liberality with which Americans always engage in any work that enlists their sympathy. As illustrative of the magnitude of this movement, it is only necessary to state that at the New York show of 1890 the St. Bernard entries numbered 151; at the Chicago show of the same year, they numbered 58; at Boston, 59; and at all the other shows the entries in this breed more than doubled in number those of any previous year.

"The total investments in St. Bernards in this country then ran into millions of dollars, and some of the choicest blood of European breeding found its way into American kennels within a few years.

"The following have been listed as among the many breeders and owners of St. Bernards in America:

Alta Kennels, Toledo, Ohio; American St. Bernard Kennels, Tomah, Wisconsin; Acme Kennels, Milwaukee, Wisconsin; H. R. Anderson, New York City; J. C. Anderson, Chattanooga, Tennessee; Alpine Kennels, New York City; C. W. Bickford, Boston Tavern, Boston, Massachusetts; Thomas Burke, Bridgeport, Connecticut; Charles T. Barney, New York City; Contoocook Kennels, Peterbor-

86

Ch. Gero-Oenz von Edelweiss (rough)
Sire: Sieger Emir v. Melina
Dam: Siegerin Erga-Oenz
Breeder: Alfred Wuthrich
Owner: J. H. Fleischli, Edelweiss Kennels.

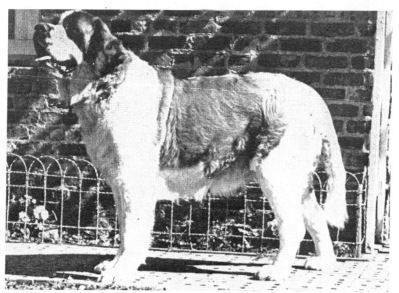

Ch. Helda v. Alpine Plateau (rough)
Sire: Ch. Felix v. Alpine Plateau   Dam: Jung Frau v. Luthy
Breeder: A. F. Hayes   Owner: Mr. Hugh Wood

87

BEAU-GESTE
Rough-Coated Male
Born January 18, 1928
(A.K.C. 650,034)

Parents	G. Parents	G.G. Parents
Sire Emir v. Altachen (A.K.C. 558,368) (S.H.S.B. 22,528)	s Dino v. Jura	s Cuno v. Jura d Kamilla v. Eistobel
	d Dana v. Sprengelbach	s Barry Oenz d Kathi v. Olten
Dam Alma Gutsch (A.K.C. 567,058) (S.H.S.B. 23,043)	s Pascha v. Drei Lillien	s Grunda v. Drei Lillien d Barry v. Gross- glockner
	d Jung Stella Gutsch	s Monch Michel Gutsch d Stella v. Eistobel

88

ough, New Hampshire; Chequasset Kennels, Lancaster, Mass.; A. Russell Crowell, Boston, Mass.; Cook Kennels, Detroit, Mich.; Dr. P. A. Dennison, Brooklyn, N. Y.; W. S. Diffendeffer, Baltimore, Md.; Lorenzo Daniels, Montclair, N. J.; Erminie Kennels, Mount Vernon, N. Y.; Elmwood Kennels, South Farmington, Mass.; George H. Eddy, Boston, Mass.; W. T. Fraser, Detroit, Mich.; Ed. H. Greiner, Buffalo, N. Y.; Halfway Brook Kennels, Glens Falls, N. Y.; Hospice Kennels, Arlington, N. J.; W. R. Huntington, Cleveland, Ohio; Mrs. H. Hughes, Joliet, Ill.; P. L. Hanscom, Oak Park, Ill.; J. C. Hobart, Chicago, Ill.; James F. Hall, Philadelphia, Pa.; Iroquois Kennels, Tonawanda, N. Y.; W. A. Joeckel, Jr., Hoboken, N. J.; John Kervan, Brooklyn, N. Y.; L. T. Kinney, Grand Rapids, Mich.; Eugene Kelmel, Boston, Mass.; Keystone Kennels, Pittsburgh, Pa.; Dr. C. A. Lougest, Jersey City, N. J.; J. B. Lewis, Belleville, Ohio; E. H. Moore, Melrose, Mass.; John Marshall, Troy, N. Y.; James Mortimer, Babylon, L. I., N. Y.; Meadowthorpe Kennels, Lexington, Ky.; Daniel Mann, New York City; Mrs. J. M. Nicholson, Albany, N. Y.; Namquoit Kennels, Boston, Mass.; Oakhurst Kennels, Chicago, Ill.; Prof. W. F. Osborne, Princeton, N. J.; Poag Kennels, Toledo, Ohio; Peninsular Kennels, Chelsea, Mich.; E. S. Pinney, Farwell House, Chicago, Ill.; A. F. Putney, Boston, Mass.; H. S. Pitkin, Hartford, Conn.; E. A. Rockwood, Buffalo, N. Y.; E. B. Sears, Melrose, Mass.; R. J. Sawyer, Menominee, Mich.; St. Gothard Kennels, Orange, N. J.; Mrs. E. E. Teague, South Farmington, Mass.; Dr. Robert Taylor, Mount Vernon, N. Y.; Trojan Kennels, Troy, N. Y.; Otto W. Volger, Buffalo, N. Y.; John G. Venn, Chicago, Ill.; John Van Velsor, Buffalo, N. Y.; Charles G. Wheelock, Arlington Heights, Mass.; G. P. Wiggin, Lawrence, Mass.; E. H. Willson, Jordan, N. Y.; Wentworth Kennels, Utica, N. Y.; Woodbrook Kennels, Baltimore, Md.

"The special characteristics of the St. Bernard are his immense size, his powerful muscular organization, his great frame, deep and broad chest, his massive head and spacious brain-pan, his heavy coat, his courage, his unswerving devotion to his human and canine friends, his kind, benevolent disposition, his sagacity and his aversion to or disregard of the attentions of strangers. Several specimens of this breed have reached a height of thirty-four inches or more at the shoulder, and a weight of two hundred pounds or over. Plinlimmon is thirty-five inches high, Sir Bedivere and Watch are each more than thirty-four inches, and many others are over thirty-three inches.

"Volumes could be filled with anecdotes and incidents of the remarkable instinct, the superior judgment, the almost human intellect, of the St. Bernard. The heroic services rendered by these dogs in rescuing and aiding snowbound travelers in the Swiss Alps are too well known to require further mention here. Hundreds of instances occurring in our own country could be cited had we the space for them. As showing the steadfast devotion of the St. Bernard for his friends, I may recall the case of a boy who was drowned in a lake in New York while skating. The body of the grand old St. Bernard dog who had been the constant companion of the boy was found at the bottom of the lake, near that of his young master, and the indications pointed plainly to the fact that the boy having broken through the ice, the dog had gone to his aid, had caught him and tried to pull him out; that the ice had broken and the dog had fallen in. Then he had released his hold, climbed out on the ice, seized his master and tried again to drag him out, but again the ice had broken. These struggles had been repeated again and again until the noble brute, exhausted by his efforts, had sunk and died by the side of his young friend."

Mr. G. W. Patterson, writing of a St. Bernard bitch that he had formerly owned, says:

"My little girl was enjoying a slide last winter, back of my house, and Sylvia was accompanying her down the hill by running alongside. When she reached the bottom of the hill, the little girl held out the rope, saying: 'Here, Sylvia, you must draw me back up the hill' and although the dog had had no training, and was only eight months old, she performed the task admirably, if not as quickly as she did afterward. Carrie never took a slide after that without having Sylvia with her to draw her back up the hill. I never could tell which enjoyed it most—both growing strong under the influence of bracing air and exercise."

It has been claimed by some of the opponents of the St. Bernard that he is dull of comprehension and difficult to train. My experience and observation teach me that such is by no means the case. I have known many St. Bernards that have been trained to perform some truly wonderful tricks, errands, and services, and that with as little time and labor as would have been necessary to train the brightest Spaniel to do the same work. Col. C. A. Swineford, of Bar-

Northeast Studios photo

Ch. Cambo v. Sauliamt (Kitto v. Sauliamt ex Tyna v. Sauliamt), owned by Theresa Betty and Janet Levine, was bred in Switzerland by Herr Eduard Rodel.

E. H. Frank Photo

Ch. Gerlo v. Sauliamt, owned by Helen Yale, is another from Herr Rodel's Sauliamt kennels. This fine rough has distinguished himself in the United States.

Canadian Ch. Baron de Beaulieu, owned by Phyllis Hodges and bred by Mr. A. Vessaz, was born in Switzerland and was sired by the celebrated C.A.C.I.B. Castor v. Leberberg.

aboo, Wisconsin, had a St. Bernard that would, at his bidding, stand on his hind feet, place his fore feet on the office railing, and walk from one end to the other of it in this position. Then, at command, he would place his hind feet on the railing, and with his fore feet on the floor, repeat the operation.

He would place his hind feet on a barrel, and standing with his fore feet on the floor, roll it back and forth across the floor. His master could send him with a note or package to any house or office where he had ever been, and the dog would return promptly with the answer. A few hours had been sufficient in which to teach the dog either of these tricks.

The St. Bernard is one of the most useful and valuable of all breeds as a watch-dog. While not vicious or savage, he is alert, coura- geous, faithful, sagacious, and his great size renders him an object of dread to wrong-doers. Few men would care to disturb property of which he had charge. Besides being an excellent guardian for chil- dren, he is also an affectionate and patient companion for them. He may not romp or run with them, but will, if harnessed and hitched to a toy wagon, draw them as faithfully and patiently as an old horse. He will allow them to ride him or impose on his good nature in almost any way they may choose, and never resent or object. Many of the noble qualities of the race are illustrated in the case of SAVE, a noted St. Bernard formerly owned in England, of which a contributor to the *American Field* wrote as follows:

"Mr. J. F. Smith mourns the loss of a dear friend and most faith- ful companion. This was Champion Save (E. 10626), one of the most notable St. Bernards ever seen. He was bred by Rev. G. A. Sneyd, being by Othman (E. 6422)—Hedwig. He was born in March, 1879, and was the only survivor of a litter of fifteen. It was on this account that he was called Save. In color and markings he was admittedly the handsomest dog ever shown here. His strength was such that he would carry his master with ease, although he weighed fourteen stone, and no two men could hold him with a chain or slip, if anyone whom he knew called him. Yet he was so gentle that the smallest child could do anything with him. He was very fond of the company of ladies, among whom he was known as Gentleman Save. He was also passionately fond of children, and delighted in their company. For some years a cot has been main- tained in the Children's Hospital, at Sheffield, solely by money col-

93

FRANZI v. EDELWEISS
Smooth Female
Born December 6, 1931
(A.K.C. 820,479)

Parents	G. Parents	G.G. Parents
Sire Ch. Barry v. Oschwand (A.K.C. 619,022)	s Barry v. Waldrand	s Sieger Emir v. Jura d Seline— (Ursenbacher)
	d Belline—Oesch	s Hektor v. Worblenthal d Belline v. Neuenegg
Dam Betty v. Edelweiss (A.K.C. 787,325)	s Ajax v. Alt-Heidelberg	s Arco v. Dreimaderlhaus d Dassy v. Freudenfels
	d Kyra v. Taubertal	s Ch. Bernd v. Mitterfels d Franzi v. Taubertal

94

lected by Save, who always carried a small cask attached to his collar. He used to go to the hospital twice a year, in January and July, to pay in his contributions, and his visits were looked for eagerly by the little ones, as all that were well enough in the ward which contained the 'Save Cot' had a ride on his back.

"He died calmly and painlessly on July third, and this grand old dog is sincerely mourned by his late owner and his family, as well as by all the children of Sheffield and many of their parents. Probably no other dog had so wide a popularity, for his portrait, first published in 1882, afterward figured in almost every illustrated journal; and the story of his life, his strength, his intelligence, his docility, and his love for children, has been told hundreds of times."

The St. Bernard has frequently been utilized as a retriever, and it is believed by many that with proper training he would excel in this class of work. A writer in the *Kennel Gazette* gives interesting and valuable testimony on this point.

CH. QUESTOR V. ALPINE PLATEAU (smooth coated dog)
Sire: Barri v. Hutwill v. Alpine Plateau   Dam: Helda v. Alpine Plateau
Breeder: A. F. Hayes   Owners: Mr. and Mrs. A. C. Boicelli

CH. GERD V.D. LUEG V. EDELWEISS (smooth coated dog)
Sire: Elmar v.d Lueg   Breeder: Ernest Grossenbacher
Dam: Bella v. Ringgeli   Owner: Mr. J. H. Fleischli

He says: "I had just put together my belongings preparatory to starting for Scotland in the evening. My friend with whom I was staying had kindly promised that during my absence he would take care of a valuable St. Bernard bitch (sister to Plinlimmon) which had recently been given to me, and, as though conscious of our impending parting, Midge, who had become greatly attached to me, lay at my feet, from time to time casting upward such beseeching glances as only our affectionate dumb pets are capable of. As the afternoon wore on, and during the early evening, the dog closely followed my every movement, almost appearing to ask that she might accompany me, until at the last moment I decided to take her.

"The first outburst of cordial greeting which welcomed me as I drove up to the house of my friend was somewhat toned down upon the appearance of my pet. I saw at once I had brought a visitor by no means popular in a sporting establishment, but trusted that time might make matters smooth; nor was I mistaken, for the dog's very

CH. FALCO-OENZ V. ALPINE PLATEAU (rough coated dog)
Sire: Ch. Gerd v.d. Lueg   Breeder: Alfred Wuthrich
Dam: Siegerin Erga-Oenz   Owners: Mr. and Mrs. R. C. Elliott
The young ladies are the daughters of Mr. and Mrs. A. C. Boicelli.

Saints get around through time and space. Bachrach took the picture, about 1930, in Concord, Mass. It shows Mrs. George P. Metcalf with ALPCRAFT EIGER. Bred by Gottlieb Zulliger, this dog was a parlay from Switzerland to Wisconsin and back to Massachusetts.

looks soon worked wonders. Days went happily by, and with Midge for my companion, I rambled by the river, rod in hand, she upon occasion leaving me to flog some pet stream while she took small hunting excursions on her own account. I noticed on several occasions that she became wondrous keen at the sound of a gun, and found one had only to raise a gun to one's shoulder to put her at once upon the alert.

"One day I had gone up to a loch for a day's trouting, and while I was thus occupied two friends went to the upper end of it in quest of ducks. It was with some difficulty that I prevented Midge from following them, and later on her uneasiness at the sound of each shot and her efforts to jump over the side of the boat gave rise to such anathemas as might well have sunk a less sturdy craft. After some time we were nearing the spot where the shooters were, and when we got to within some three or four hundred yards of them a duck was duly brought down, at sight of which Midge broke away from me, swam to the bird, a considerable distance, retrieved it in perfect form, without disturbing a feather.

"Later in the day other chances presented themselves, the results being always satisfactory, and especially so in one or two instances where a less powerful dog would have been utterly unequal to making his way through the thick reeds and sedge. Now, to me it seems that with very little training these really well-bred St. Bernards might be most useful in the field in such situations as I have mentioned, and over heavy, marshy ground, and I send the above account, not desiring to claim more for them than they deserve, but to meet the assertions many people make that these large dogs are treacherous and useless pets to have about a place. I may, in conclusion, say that to her other accomplishments Midge adds that of poacher-hunting, having on one occasion knocked down and held a man until the keeper with whom she had gone out on the quest came up; and the prisoner was only too glad to surrender his arms and accouterments on condition of the dog being called off, though she had not bitten him, but had merely held him down by the moral persuasion of a pair of heavy paws and an ominous growl when he attempted to move."

American and Canadian Ch. Treu v. Meister (Mt. Sneffels Murgatroyd ex Kathja v. Bernhardiner Hof), owned by Bruce and Marilyn Chapman.

The St. Bernard in America to Mid-Century

by Mrs. Henry H. Hubble

I SHALL attempt in this chapter to give a brief outline of the history of the Saint Bernard in America. I shall point out the highlights of the Saint Bernard Club of America's activities since its origin, mention briefly some of the most outstanding bloodlines of the past, and lastly and most important, discuss some of the more outstanding dogs of today together with their bloodlines and who owns them.

Introduction to America

The exact origin of the Saint Bernard fancy in America is not known. We do know, however, that some time around 1880 the Saint Bernard or a large dog called by that name was introduced to American theater audiences.

CH. TERENCE OF SUNNY SLOPE:, bred by Howard Parker and owned by Mrs. Nancy Wright.

Founding of the Breed Club

The later 1880's, namely 1887 and 1888, were very important years for the Saint Bernard breed in both this country and Europe. It was in June, 1887, in Zurich, Switzerland, that the international congress was held to establish a standard for the Saint Bernard breed. The Swiss standard of the breed was adopted and called the International Standard.

In the year 1888, a group of Americans met and organized the Saint Bernard Club of America. On February 22 of that year, they adopted the International Standard established by the Zurich congress to govern the breed in this country. It should be noted that all countries except England accepted the International Standard.

As one might expect, the above conditions established the basis for a great and long continued controversy in this country because the adopted standard was not compatible with the then more prominent in America, English type Saint Bernard. However, at that time most of the American owners were content with the English type dog, since the majority of their dogs had come from England. We know that the original club was still operating in the year 1892 because in May of that year a small booklet containing the adopted standard, constitution and by-laws of the club as well as the membership roster was published. In this publication 68 members were listed.

The officers and governors of the club at that time were as follows: W. H. Joeckel, Jr., Bloomfield, N. J., president; Miss Anna H. Whitney, Lancaster, Mass.; R. J. Sawyer, Menominee, Mich., and Jacob Ruppert, Jr., New York, N. Y., vice presidents; E. B. Sears, Melrose, Mass., treasurer; and J. C. Thurston, New York, N.Y., secretary.

Other governors were:

William C. Rieck, New York, N. Y.; R. T. Rennie, Newark, N. J.; W. A. Wells, Brooklyn, N. Y.; F. H. Moore, Melrose, Mass.; B. P. Johnson, New York, N. Y.; K. E. Hopf, Arlington, N. J.; W. H. Walbridge, Peterborough, N. H.; Otto W. Volger, Buffalo, N. Y.; and I. A. Sibley, address unknown.

Nothing more is heard of the club until December 30, 1897, when ten men journeyed to Grand Rapids, Michigan, to organize another Saint Bernard Club of America. The meeting was held in the office of Dudley E. Waters, who from that time until his death on January 19, 1931, served as secretary-treasurer of the Club.

The minutes of this Grand Rapids session make no mention of any previous Saint Bernard Club of America, but the constitution and by-laws adopted were substantially the same as those drawn up by the original club. Again, the International Standard was approved and adopted, and a new slate of officers and governors elected. The new club started off with a charter membership of 58.

Col. Jacob Ruppert, Jr., was elected president and Mr. Waters was named secretary-treasurer. The ten men who attended this second organization meeting were George P. Savage, Spring Lake, Mich.; W. S. Hall, Grand Rapids; R. L. Hills, New York, N. Y.; B. C. Cobb, Grand Rapids; W. G. McKennan, Sioux Falls, S.D.; Nat Robbins, Grand Haven, Mich.; W. O. Hughart, Jr., Grand Rapids; Mr. Waters, A. W. Hine and Fred McCarthy, all of Grand Rapids.

103

1970 DOG HERO OF THE YEAR

POLAR BLU SAMARITAN VON BARRI with his owner, Mrs. Theresa Gratias, of Achorage, Alaska. This rough coated male is known affectionately as "Grizzly Bear," and has been awarded the 1970 Dog Hero of the Year Award.

The 175-pound dog saved his mistress from a possible severe mauling when she inadvertently came between a real grizzly bear, a female, and the bear's cub.

Mrs. Gratias had stepped from her cabin when she almost tripped over the cub. When she turned to flee back toward the cabins' only door, the cub's mother was between her and escape. Quickly turning away, Mrs. Gratias slipped on a patch of ice and fell. The bear attacked, grabbing Mrs. Gratias by the arm. Then the Saint attacked and drove the enraged sow toward the woods and away from his mistress, who had fainted. Regaining consciousness, Mrs. Gratias found herself on the front porch of her cabin under the watchful eye of her Saint Bernard. Mrs. Gratias was scratched and bitten. The blood on her dog turned out to be the bear's. Her dog was unharmed.

104

Following secretary-treasurer Waters' death in 1931, Mr. M. T. Vanden Bosch of Grand Rapids acted in his place and assisted in the re-organization of the Saint Bernard Club of America for the second time in its history.

In March of 1932 Mr. Joseph T. Mulray of Newtown Square, Pennsylvania, and Mr. Leroy E. Fess of Williamsville, N. Y., served as the re-organization battery in the capacity of president and secretary-treasurer, respectively. The re-organized officers were in charge of the Club's affairs to February 13, 1933, when the first meeting was held at the Hotel Victoria, New York City. The Club then began to function on the "mail-order basis." In the New York meeting the officers and governors of the Club were elected and took office. The Saint Bernard Club of America again took its seat among the American Kennel Club's big family of specialty clubs.

CH. GERO CHRISTOPHER of Skycroft was reported to be the top winning rough coat Saint Bernard in breed history, with 7 Bests in Show, 22 Working Group 1sts, 17 Working Group 2nds, 15 Working Group 3rds, 6 Working Group 4ths and 84 Bests of Breed. Breeder: Shirlie C. Cox. Owners: Shirlie C. Cox and Ann E. Humphreys. Born: October 1, 1960.

Sire: Ch. Caesar of Coca Hill   Dam: Brandy of Skycroft

105

CH. PRARIEAIRE ROX V. ZWING-BASKO (Ch. Basko von Salmegg ex Hilltops Honey Baby Zwingo), owned by Winifred Martin, has proven himself a top stud dog with a good number of champion offspring and others with points.

The officers and governors elected in the New York meeting were as follows: President, Joseph H. Fleischli, Springfield, Ill.; Vice Presidents, Paul R. Forbriger, William Gartner, Paul G. Tilenius, all of Brooklyn, N. Y.; Secretary-Treasurer, Mrs. Eleanor J. Dalton, Stamford, Conn.; Governors, Eleanor Cavanagh, Eleanor J. Dalton, Joseph H. Fleischli, Paul R. Forbriger, Alice H. French, William Gartner, Arthur Hesser, Agnes Kemp, Joseph T. Mulray, Robert Nicholson, Jessyn S. Robinson, Paul G. Tilenius, Leo C. Urlaub, Gottlieb Zulliger.

The Saint Bernard Club of America had been inactive for a long period between the years 1897 and 1932, during which time the breed was greatly degenerated. This degeneration was due primarily to the fact that there was no organized effort to maintain and improve the quality of the breed in this country, and many of the dogs were bred by "dog dealers" instead of by persons having a full knowledge of the breed or having its best interest at heart.

About the time of the re-organization of the Club in 1932, and shortly prior to that date, several Saint Bernard fanciers in the United States imported Swiss and German bred Saint Bernards. These dogs were then used for breeding purposes, and a revitalization of the breed was started.

Breed Progress 1932-1945

I should like to mention a few of the outstanding dogs which were used in the comeback for the breed. These individuals are the basis for the bloodlines which were most prominent in the United States in the late 1930's and up to 1945. Prominent among the Saint Bernard Dogs imported after World War I, listed in chronological order, are the following:

Kavalier vom Grossglockner	rough German Champion
Nanni Deppeler	rough Swiss bitch
Barry von Oschwand	rough Swiss dog
Pluto von Altachen	rough Swiss dog
Tasso von Goppingen	rough German dog
Lola vom Rigi	smooth Swiss bitch
Rasko v.d. Reppisch	rough Swiss Sieger and international Champion

Berna v.d. Lueg	rough Swiss bitch
Dora Belmont	rough Swiss bitch
Odschi von Margothof	rough German bitch
Varus vom Grossglockner	rough German dog
Nero von Multenrain	rough Swiss dog
Tell von Lotten	rough Swiss dog
Rigo vom Rigi	smooth Swiss dog
Palace vom Rigi	smooth Swiss bitch
Vallo vom Rigi	smooth Swiss Sieger
Porthos von Falkenstein	rough German dog
Cid von Eiger	rough Swiss dog
Doldi vom Grossglockner	rough German dog
Esbo vom Grossglockner	rough German dog
Apollo von Rougang	rough Swiss Sieger
Armin v.d. Teck	smooth German dog

As individual specimens, most of the dogs imported were of good type and were able to contribute a great deal to the build-up of a more correct American Saint Bernard.

Importance of Smooth Breeding Stock

Most of the above individuals listed, as you will note, were rough coated. By examination of their pedigrees,. one will find that all of those which are of an outstanding character and quality had a considerable amount of smooth blood in their immediate pedigrees. This is a very, very important factor in the continued breeding of the correct-type Saint Bernard, and has been recognized as a primary law of breeding by the noted authorities of Switzerland and Germany for many, many years. As one might expect, therefore, the continued breeding of rough to rough dogs resulted in a gradual degeneration of type. It was necessary from time to time to have importation of new primary stock from Switzerland or Germany, which had been developed from the breeding practices using some smooth coated dogs. After the start of World War II it was impossible to import any new stock; therefore, the loss of correct type was somewhat accelerated during those years.

The phenomena back of the fact that type is lost so rapidly by continued breeding of only the rough coated dogs without any

CH. HARRY NO BUDDY, owned by Mr. and Mrs. C. Westcott Gallup, Jr., of Wayne, Illinois. Mrs. Gallup is handling her dog in this photograph. "Harry" was top winning Saint Bernard in America 1965-1966 and fourth of all Working Dogs in America in 1966. His wins include 119 Bests of Breed, 24 Group firsts, 86 Group placings and a Best in Show. This rough coated male has sired seven champions to date.

Sire: Ch. MaBobs Buddy v. Mighty Moe   Dam: Ch. Zwinghof Quinet v. Zwingo
Whelped: February 8, 1963

refreshment by the smooth individuals is not fully understood; but it is a proven fact, one that has been demonstrated repeatedly in England and America. Regardless of how carefully the selection of progeny is made, this loss of type does occur. It was therefore a very noteworthy event when soon after the cessation of hostilities in Europe American breeders started the importation of new blood. It was even more important for the benefit of the American Saint Bernard that many of these imports were of the smooth variety, because this meant that we then had available in the United States the important smooth coated strains for the continued revitalization of the breed.

The majority of the imports since 1945 have been smooth coated Saint Bernards. We have had both males and females brought to this country, which is a very important point because this makes it possible to breed the true smooth lines without any dilution of the bloodline. In the forthcoming portions of this chapter, I shall discuss the various individual dogs which have been imported and give present owners' names of these dogs for the benefit of those persons interested in using them for breeding or obtaining this stock. It is

ALFA DU HOSPICE DU SIMPLON (Switzerland) and little Lisa Tanen (New Mexico) get acquainted near Alfa's new home in America.
Sire: Jeckar v. Sauliamt   Dam: Brunetta v Marktplatz   Born: June 6, 1967
Owner: Jan Cooper, Santa Fe, New Mexico

110

This photograph of CH. LION D'OR was chosen from many others as it is the best picture the editors have of Laurence Powell, former President of the Saint Bernard Club of America. Mr. Powell has shown many Saints to their championships, including five generations of title-holders.

not enough that a few good dogs be imported and used for breeding with existing stock, but these imported dogs must be interbred in the correct manner if real progress as to individual specimen quality is to be made in this country. There are many cases where such breeding is being carried out today and the results are most excellent. In short, the American Saint Bernard has never been in a more favorable position than he is today. There are a considerable number of direct imports of the highest quality and a large number of American-bred progeny of these dogs which are exhibiting the fine qualities of their ancestors. The smooth coated variety has become well established in the eyes of the breed fanciers who are interested in showing and breeding, as well as in the eyes of the general public, many of whom had not seen the smooth variety in this country before 1946.

I do not want to make it appear that the rough coated Saint Bernard should be dropped, or should not be considered an important type dog; but if the rough dog is to attain the highest possible status, it is by the correct breeding of roughs with smooths to establish the desired medium.

Leading Saint Bernards in the United States

In discussing the dogs and the kennels of the United States, I shall discuss only the recently imported bloodlines and a few of their immediate offspring. These are, in my opinion, the bases for the American Saint Bernard of the future.

Discussion of various breeders and their dogs is arranged by geographical location, starting on the east coast of the United States and progressing westward.

East Coast Breeders

On the east coast we have some very fine dogs and some top quality breeding in progress today. The Sunny Slopes Kennels of Mr. and Mrs. Howard P. Parker, Webbs Hill Road, Stamford, Conn., have two of our most prized Swiss imports, Swiss Siegerin Fortuna vom Rigi and her brother Champion Falco vom Rigi C.D. Both of these smooth coated dogs came from the world-famous Swiss Rigi Kennels, owner Carl Steiner, representing the hospice type Saint

Roy photo

On his seventh birthday, CH. SANCTUARY WOODS GULLIVER poses between challenge trophies won at the Pacific Coast specialty show by son Fantabulous and daughter Nita Nanette.

Bernard. Fortuna vom Rigi won the much coveted Swiss Siegerin title at 18 months and is the only bitch ever to reach our shores having this, the highest Saint Bernard title of excellence.

These dogs have been used for breeding and each has produced excellent progeny. Mr. and Mrs. Parker have raised Saint Bernards for many years and their Sunny Slopes Kennels contain many top quality Saints. Mrs. Parker has gained eminence in the field of obedience training of Saint Bernards. Dogs of her training have won several C.D. degrees and at least one C.D.X. degree in obedience trials.

Mr. Kurt Diedrich, Allendale, N. J., is the owner of the beautiful smooth coated son of Falco vom Rigi, named Diedrich's Armin, whose dam is Bella v. Sabesi, a Swiss type smooth bitch.

Mr. Stanley H. Bussinger, owner of Highmont Kennels, Philadelphia, Pa., is the owner of two excellent imported smooth Saint Bernards, Minka v. Immenberg and Champion Major v. Neu-Habsburg. Major was imported by Mr. Frank Maxwell, Lake Stockholm, N. J., and is a son of Fata vom Rigi (litter sister of Fortuna vom Rigi owned by Mr. and Mrs. H. P. Parker) and Hector V. Zwing Uri. As an example of the excellent breeding being carried out in the East, Fortuna was bred to Major, this litter representing line breeding of the highest caliber. Minka v. Immenberg is sired by Hasso v. Zwing-Uri, litter brother of Hector v. Zwing-Uri. Minka's dam is Nelda v.d. Lohnmatt, whose sire is Hector v.d. Lohnmatt and is out of Belline (Schar).

Mr. Victor Bittermann, owner of Peekamoose Kennels, West Shokan, Ulster Co., N. Y., has imported a fine German bitch Katja v. Ludwigstein.

Midwest Breeders

In the midwest we have one of the oldest and most widely known kennels in the United States. The Edelweiss Kennels, owned by Mr. Joseph H. Fleischli, Springfield, Ill., were founded by Franz Fleischli, and is now operated by his son, Joseph H. Fleischli, who has raised Saint Bernards since 1908. Mr. Fleischli has imported an imposing number of excellent Saint Bernards from Switzerland and Germany during the many years of operating his kennel. Recent Swiss imports which are presently owned by Mr. Fleischli are the

CH. SANCTUARY WOODS FANTABULOUS, a multiple best-in-show winner, is at home here with owner Beatrice Knight in his native Oregon hills. A more formal picture of the famous Fantabulous was selected to represent his breed in the book, *Visualization of the Standards.*

Two delightful and apparently delighted three-month-old female Saints with owner Anne Mann. At the left is the rough, THE ABBEY'S HAPPY BOTTOM and at the right the smooth, THE ABBEY'S Q-T PIE.

116

outstanding Champion Gerd v.d. Lueg v. Edelweiss, winner of 17 Best in Shows, Champion Gero-Oenz v. Edelweiss and Bella v. Menzberg.

Bella v. Menzberg's sire is Champion Gerd v.d. Lueg v. Edelweiss out of Freya v. Emmenschachen, whose sire is Faro v. Schmidigen and out of Alma v. Bornfeld.

Gerd v.d. Lueg and Gero-Oenz were used widely at stud and contributed greatly to the improvement of the Saint Bernard breed in the United States. There are also several Swiss-bred sons and daughters of Gerd which have been imported to this country.

Mr. Hubert Heilman, Vermillion, Ohio, is the owner of Champion Aline v.d. Roth, an imported smooth daughter of Gerd v.d. Alpine Plateau (sired by the smooth Swiss import Barri v. Huttwil v. Alpine Plateau). She has produced an excellent litter sired by Gerd v.d. Lueg.

Mr. John M. Friend, Hartland, Wisc., owns the imported smooth male Champion Also v.d. Roth, litter brother of the previous mentioned Aline v.d. Roth.

In the Kennels of Odessa Llewllyn, Waukee, Iowa, we have the rough coated Swiss import Champion Joggi-Oenz v. Edelweiss. He is the same breeding as Gero-Oenz v. Edelweiss; however, from a later litter.

To the best of my knowledge these are all the direct imports in the Midwest today; however, there are numerous other kennels which have been using the above imports to improve their bloodlines. A few such kennels are: Janday Kennels, owned by Mr. and Mrs. Archie Shea, Columbus, Ohio; Carl-Criss Kennels, owned by Mr. and Mrs. Carl E. Fritts, Tulsa, Okla.; and Wedigston Kennels, owned by Dr. Henry E. Wedig, Newtown, Ohio.

West Coast Breeders

The first kennel I should like to discuss on the west coast is one which unfortunately is not operating at this time; however, due to its great influence on the breed in the country today, it should be discussed in detail. The Alpine Plateau Kennels of Mr. and Mrs. A. F. Hayes, formerly of Portland, Oregon, were responsible for the importation of several excellent Swiss-bred Saint Bernards which have contributed greatly to the breed's improvement and recognition in the United States.

To Mr. Harold Jarvis, San Francisco, Calif., goes the honor of importing the first Swiss-bred Saint Bernard to the United States after World War II. His import was the smooth bitch Champion Horsa v. Zwing Uri, C.D., a very fine specimen of the breed. Like Falco v. Rigi, Horsa made C.D. under Mrs. H. P. Parker.

Mr. Don Diessner, Yakima, Washington, imported another of the much-sought-after Rigi-bred Saints from the kennel of Mr. Carl Steiner, the smooth bitch Mira vom Rigi. Mira is sired by Hector v. Zwing-Uri, who is by the Sieger Nero v. Zwing-Uri out of Siegerin Alma v. Reitnau. Mira's dam is Hertha v. Rigi, who was sired by Astor v. Reitnau out of Siegerin Berna v. Rigi.

A few of the others on the West Coast having American-bred Saint Bernards of the above bloodlines are:

1. Mrs. Beatrice Knight, owner of the Sanctuary Woods Kennels, Drain, Oregon.

2. Mr. and Mrs. Hugh B. Woods, owners of Ridgewood Acres Kennels, Eugene, Oregon.

3. Mr. and Mrs. Adolph Boicelli, San Francisco, California.

4. Mr. and Mrs. E. J. Van Matre, owners of Ima Kennels, Pleasanton, California.

Historical note from the editors

Mr. and Mrs. Hubble were themselves well-known western breeders. In the years since this chapter was written, history-minded members of the fancy have concerned themselves with the question, "Who got there first in North America?" There are many different ways to answer this question.

The first Saint Bernard kennel to be registered with the American Kennel Club was probably Carmen Kennel, operated by T. E. L. Kemp, of Bridgewater, Mass., and licensed on April 22, 1903. Mr. Kemp, one of the first professional photographers, interested himself in taking pictures of horses, then dogs, especially Saint Bernards, then founded an early dog show organization which ran the first Eastern Dog Club show. His wife, Agnes, became the first all-rounder woman judge. His daughter, now Mrs. Harold Holmes, with her husband, continues to operate Carmen Kennel, which establishes something of a record for continuous devotion to the breed.

Franz Fleischli came from Luzerne, Switzerland and founded the

118

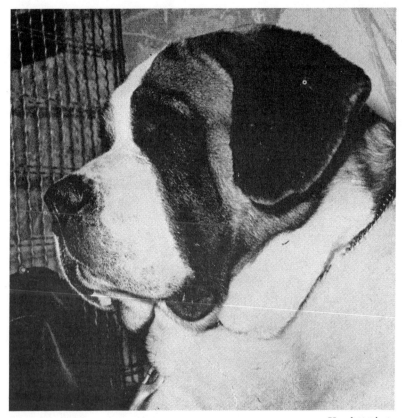

CH. SANCTUARY WOODS BETTER TIMES, smooth coated male. An all-time great showman, "Old Timer" was awarded 10 Best in Show wins and 23 Firsts in Group. His show record and beauty have earned him a permanent home in the hearts of true fanciers.

CH. KOBI VON STEINHERNHOF, owned by C. M. Cawker of Foxboro, Ontario. Kobi's breeder was Hans Zimmerli, of Langenthal, for many years president of the St. Bernard Breeders' Association of Switzerland. Mr. Cawker has done much to bring to the Canadian scene a St. Bernard which was truly a member of the Working group.

Since this picture was taken, Kobi completed his American championship and became, it is believed, the first Canadian Saint ever to hold titles in both countries. He was also busy at home, and at the latest count had sired 350 puppies.

Edelweiss Kennel, in Springfield, Illinois, about 1894. His son, Joseph, continued to raise Saints, founded an important dog magazine and dog book company, and wrote one of the first books on Saint Bernards, early editions of which are treasured by fanciers. Edelweiss is a name of special significance to Swiss and Austrians, and the Fleischlis, father and son, are of special significance to Saints.

Gottlieb Zulliger, from Canton Bern, Switzerland, has been preoccupied with Saints for about seventy years, which may make him the longevity champion of the breed. By profession a cheesemaker, Mr. Zulliger traveled through Europe and the United States, finally reaching Monroe, Wisconsin, where he began the Alpcraft Kennel in about 1910. Monroe, primarily a Swiss colony, became the source of many fine Saints. Gottlieb and his wife, Rose, were retiring at the time of the 1963 edition.

Frasie photo

CH. HARVEY'S ZWINGO BARRI VON BANZ, owner-handler Grace Harvey, and some of the tangible rewards for a best-in-show winner. Mrs. Harvey is more proud of Zwingo's success as a fine family dog than of his consistent win record.

The St. Bernard in North America into the 1970's

THE Saint Bernard population in North America exploded during the 1960's. Ten years ago the breed was regarded as one of the "rare breeds." The 1970 American Kennel Club statistics ranked the Saint Bernard as number twelve in popularity of all registrable breeds, based on number of registrations.

The Saint Bernard has held a certain mystique all through his history. The reputation the breed enjoys as a result of heroic exploits accomplished during the time he was "King of the Alps" fans the imagination of the public. The affluence enjoyed by many during the late 50's and early 60's made it possible for more potential dog owners to consider purchasing a giant breed. As the demand increased, the number of breeders increased until it is no longer possible to compile an accurate listing of all the small, medium or large scale breeders.

Breed Clubs

As interest in the breed grew, so did interest in learning more

122

CH. RUDE'S HI JINKS v. BUSTER—(smooth)

"Hi Jinks" became the top winning Saint Bernard in America in 1968 and top winning bitch of all time with 98 Best of Breed wins, 75 Group placings, BOB—National Specialty 1968, BOB—Northern Illinois Specialty 1968, BOB—Indiana Specialty 1967, two BOS—National Specialty 1966-1967, and one Best in Show award. "Jinks" is owned by Mr. Stanley Rude. Above, Mr. Dick Cooper is handling her to Best in Show under Judge Derek Rayne at the Central Florida Kennel Club.

about the breed by new fanciers. New area clubs were organized all over North America which included Alaska, Hawaii and Canada. The membership of the Saint Bernard Club of America increased from approximately 300 in 1960 to 800 by 1970.

As a member club of the American Kennel Club, the Saint Bernard Club of America is the custodian of the Saint Bernard Standard and the organization with which all other clubs organized specifically for the benefit of the Saint Bernard must be affiliated to gain show-holding privileges.

The Saint Bernard Club of America is called the "Parent Club." Clubs formed regionally specifically for the benefit of the Saint Bernard are called "breed clubs" or "specialty clubs." After an area breed club has been organized, it may apply to the parent club for affiliation. For details and specifics on club organization readers may contact any of the clubs listed below.

The following listing of breed clubs affiliated with the Saint Bernard Club of America will provide a means for enthusiasts to contact others interested in the breed. Secretaries often change from year to year. In the event such change delays correspondence, the American Kennel Club will forward inquiries upon request.

Even as this is being written new clubs are forming and requesting affiliation with the parent club. Your letter addressed to the American Kennel Club or the parent club requesting club information or breeder listings will be forwarded to the club nearest to your home unless otherwise specified.

American Kennel Club	The Canadian Kennel Club
51 Madison Avenue	111 Eglinton Ave. E.
New York, New York 10010	Toronto 12, Ontario, Canada

(Editor's Note: In interest of brevity, the initials S.B.C. are used in place of a full spelling out of Saint Bernard Club)

Apple Valley S.B.C.	Central Florida S.B.C.
Mr. Herbert H. Zorat	Rt. 1, Box 399
8 North 12th St.	Anne Mann
Selah, Washington 98492	Odessa, Florida 33556

Central Indiana S.B.C.	Eastern Virginia S.B.C.
Barbara Van Osch	Barbara Adams
127 W. Grant St.	4952 Woodland Drive
Lynn, Indiana 43755	Chesapeake, Va. 23701

CH. FREIDA'S AL-VER-DON-FRAUSTY, sire of 16 champions. One of his daughters, Ch. Nelda of Birchwood, was dam of 22 champions. A son, Ch. Bowser Waller, below, has sired seven champions.

CH. BOWSER WALLER, Smooth male. His show record: 100 Bests of Breed, 60 Group placings and five Best in Show wins. Bowser placed in the top ten for Saint Bernards for five consecutive years. He has sired seven champions to date.

Four State S.B. Association
Bill Summers
501 E. 28th
Pittsburg, Kansas 66762

Fort Worth-Dallas S.B.C.
Don Gill
11135 Shortmeadow Lane
Dallas, Texas 75218

Great Plains S.B.C.
Marverne Wurst
308 5th Street
Milford, Nebraska 68405

Greater Iowa S.B.C.
Maxine Smith
1307-8th Ave. N.E.
Independence, Iowa 50644

Greater Madison S.B.C.
Mrs. Nancy Womack
4000 Dempsey Road
Madison, Wisc. 53716

Greater Milwaukee S.B.C.
Sandra Reuter
1098 View Road
Madison, Wisc. 53711

Greater Twin Cities S.B.C.
John Turbitt
7948 Penn Ave. N.
Minneapolis, Minn. 55430

Heart of America S.B.C.
Joyce Collins
2502 E. 63rd Place N.
Gladstone, Mo. 64118

Middle Atlantic S.B.C
Sandra Saybolt
R.D.
Glen Moore, Penn. 19343

New England S.B.C.
Gail Devine
P.O. Box 357, Mason Rd.
Chatham, N. Y. 12037

Northeast Maryland S.B.C.
Betty Boulden
P.O. Box 66
Newark, Delaware 19711

Northern Colorado S.B.C.
Diane McHatton
7459 Knox Ct.
Westminster, Colo. 80030

Northern Illinois S.B.C.
Gloria Wallin
Rt. 1, Box 289
Gren Bay Rd., Zion, Ill. 60099

Northern New Jersey S.B.C.
Vera Hyman
620 Jones Road
Englewood, N. J. 07631

Kalamazoo S.B.C.
Gail Teller
3019 Sonora
Kalamazoo, Mich. 49004

Ohio S.B.C.
Verla Roberts
1909 Rosemont Avenue
Columbus, Ohio 43223

Presque Isle S.B.C.
Carol Ward
1745½ Clifford Drive
Erie, Penn. 16506

Sacramento-Sierra S.B.C.
Janice Dees
Rt. 1, Box 226
Galt, Calif. 95632

CH. CAREY'S ACE OF FANTABULOUS, owned and handled by Cliff Nippress. "Ace" was bred by John J. Carey. Sire: Ch. Sanctuary Woods Fantabulous Dam: Bubbling Over of Four Winds.

American and Canadian CH. VIELEDANKE GOMBU, owned by J. T. and T. B. Thank. "Gombu" was bred by Pearl N. Thank.
Sire: Ch. Sanctuary Woods Gulliver
Dam: Tyrolia.

Seattle S.B.C.
Jim Cooley
18827 Midvale N.
Seattle, Wash. 98133

S.B.C. of Greater Wash. D. C.
John Roose
6008 Jennings Lane
Springfield, Va. 22150

S.B.C. of Greater New York
Mrs. John Heck
Half Moon Hollow Road
Ridge, N. Y. 11961

S.B.C. of the Pacific Coast
Diane Fies
153 Cherokee Way
Portola Valley, Calif. 94025

S.B.C. of San Diego
Dalene Overmire
Rt. 1, Box 960
Escondido, Calif. 92025

S.B.C. of Puget Sound
Nina G. Echols
Rt. 7, Box 7335
Bainbridge Island, Wash. 98110

S.B.C. of Western Oregon
Krista Reed
13545 S. W. Walker
Beaverton, Oregon 97005

S.B.C. of Southern California
Diane Night
11764 Laurel Crest Drive
Studio City, Calif. 91604

S.B. Fanciers Association
Mr. J. Terhorst
10424 Thrush Avenue
Fountain Valley, Calif. 92708

S.B.C. of Southern Florida
Jeanne Hackman
16920 S.W. 121 Avenue
Miami, Florida 33157

S.B.C. of Greater Atlanta
Mrs. H. R. Stephens, Jr.
2625 Old Norcross Road
Tucker, Ga. 30084

S.B.C. of Michigan
Terry Kenifeck
9801 Gibbs Road
Clarkston, Mich. 48016

S.B.C. of Birmingham
Bettie Falter
Rt. 1, Box 296
McCalla, Ala. 35111

S.B.C. of Greater Detroit
Camilla Thorne
2022 Rush Lake Rd.
R.D. 3, Pickney, Mich. 48169

S.B.C. of Middle Tennessee
Evie Todd
143 Brookfield Drive
Nashville, Tenn. 37205

S.B.C. of Greater Buffalo
Mary Anne Kustra
97 Amber Street
Buffalo, New York 14220

S.B.C. of New Orleans
Robert A. Jensen
2813 Laplace Street
New Orleans, La. 70043

Southern Oregon S.B.C.
Barbara Dickson
15852 Ramsey Road
Central Point, Oregon 97501

Ch. Ma-Bob's Moe Buddy v. Buddy.

Ch. Zwinghof Golden Eagle v. Jumbo.

Ch. Zwinghof Aiming Hi Back-Jumbo.

CH. HEILMAN'S KATY von GERO

Sire: Ch. Gero-Oenz von Edelweiss   Dam: Ch. Maida v. Alpine Plateau

Owners: Mr. and Mrs. Donald Grave

"Katy" is pictured here with three challenge trophies she held at the same time, two of which she retired, having won them both three times: The St. Bernard Club of Pacific Coast Ma Keaton Trophy and the St. Bernard Club of Southern California Carl Spitz Trophy. At the 1959 Specialty Show of the St. Bernard Club of the Pacific Coast, Katy's son, Ch. Apollo v. Lion D'Or took Best of Breed, Katy was Best Opposite Sex and her daughter, Ginger, was Winners Bitch.

S.B.C. of Greater St. Louis
A. Dabbs
P.O. Box 142
Edwardsville, Ill. 62025

S.B. Fanciers of Orange County
Blanche Carey
2473 West 255th St.
Lomita, Calif. 90717

S.B.C. of Greater Phoenix
Helen Anderson
1111 West Turney Avenue
Phoenix, Arizona 85013

Tri-Counties S.B.C.
Lorne Faulkner
2265 James Avenue
Ventura, Calif. 93003

S.B.C. of Albuquerque
Mrs. Phyllis Collier
Box 266
Tijeras, New Mexico

The International View

Hundreds of dedicated fanciers go to Europe every year in search of a fine specimen for show, to add to their breeding stock or simply to bring home as a beautiful family pet. Many of these North American travellers wish to attend dog shows while they are abroad.

As an aid for those planning a trip abroad, or for those fanciers who would like to become better acquainted with Saint breeders in other countries through correspondence, we offer the following list:

The Saint Bernard Club of Switzerland
Herr B. Hagenbuch
8911 Oberlunkhofen, Switzerland

The Saint Bernard Club of Holland
Mrs. A. Cloo-de-Vries
Nijelamer (Fr.) Holland

The Saint Bernard Club of Germany
Mr. E. Schmitt
6 Frankfurt/Rodelsheim
Alexander Str. 46, Germany

The Saint Bernard Club of Scotland
Mrs. Judith McMurray
Pentire, 52 Irving Road
Kilmarnock, Ayshire, Scotland

On the bench at Chicago International, reading from left to right, are ZWINGHOF JEANNEN VON XESBO, GEORGE M. HARVEY, II, and CH. ZWINGHOF JUMBO VON XESBO. The scene is typical of the Saint Bernard benches at a dog show, which seem to be occupied by almost as many children as dogs.

132

The Saint Bernard Club of France
Mr. Fabre
Cours Pierre-Puget
Marseilles 66, France

The Saint Bernard Club of Italy
Dr. Antonio Morsiani
Villa Morsiani
48010 Bagnara di Romagna
Ravenna, Italy

The Saint Bernard Club of Denmark
Miss Ingrid Andreason
Fr. Sundsvej 26
Stenloese, Denmark

The Saint Bernard Club of Finland
Maj. Lis Ehnbert
Palokunnatie 33
Laaksolahti, Finland

The Saint Bernard Club of Norway
Mrs. Lars Bjornsrud
Heggedal, Norway

The Saint Bernard Club of Sweden
Mr. August V. Lundgren Ing.
Lister-Mjallby, Sweden

The Show Ring

During this period of breed history, competition in the show ring is reflecting the result of swift population growth and keen breeder competition.

In some areas of America during the 1950's and 1960's it was difficult to find enough competition in Saint Bernard entries to bring a dog to its championship. That was especially true in the deep South and in the Midwest. The East and West coasts enjoyed more breed popularity in 1960 and, consequently, keener competition and larger entries in the show ring.

As interest in breeding and showing was renewed in the Midwest and spread into the South during the 1960's, breed entries became more equalized at all-breed and specialty club shows all over America. It is no longer unusual to find regular all-breed shows with Saint Bernard entries of 20 to 100. In 1969 and 1970 the annual Northern Illinois Saint Bernard Club Specialty Show had an entry exceeding 300 Saints.

Importing

The more affluent economy of the 1950's and 1960's, coupled with jet travel, led to increasing importation of Saint Bernards from European countries into North America.

Smooth or Rough?

Surveys conducted during the 1960's by the Saint Bernard Club of America have shown that the majority of smooths have been bred and shown on the West and East coasts. During the breeding career of Mr. Joseph Fleischli (discussed elsewhere in this book), the smooth was highly respected in the Midwest. But between the time Mr. Fleischli ceased breeding and the mid-1960's, there were very few serious breeders in the Midwest and those seemed not to prefer the smooth. It may or may not be coincidental that a rekindling of interest for the smooth in the Midwest occurred during the fabulous show career of the beautiful smooth show bitch, Ch. Rude's Hi Jinks. There is a healthy balance of both coat types on the Western and Eastern coasts. The breed standard clearly indicates that the smooth and rough are identical except for coat type.

Conclusion

With monthly registrations of the Saint Bernard regularly going over 1,000, plus the enthusiasm for importing specimens as show stock, breeding stock and for pets, the Saint Bernard sport should continue to be one of vast interest for some time to come.

If there is to be an overview of all the activity within the breed to this point in time, it might be that within the show rings of America there are to be found specimens the equal of Gero, Gerd, and Rasko. The greats will always remain great and the pattern for

134

American and Canadian CH. BEAU CHEVAL'S MT. LESA MARDOUG (Ch. Illo Vom Vogelheim ex Ch. Beau Cheval's Mountain Alisia), owned by Bruce and Marilyn Chapman and bred by Marlene Anderson.

future generations to follow and improve upon, as no dog has been faultless. There are many Saint Bernards of poor quality, many of good quality, a few of excellent quality and, then, the rare great. It has always been that way. From the many come the few.

Recommended Reading

As dog fanciers seek for definitive knowledge, researchers answer. New knowledge and information stemming from intense research in the fields of canine medicine, canine nutrition, canine behavior,

Sirlin photo

"Beggar," from Sacramento, California, and three-year-old Bobby Mitchell both lived to have their picture taken because Beggar pulled Bobby out of the flooded American River in May of 1962. Beggar was judged "dog hero of the year" as a result.

canine genetics, and breeding practice makes any effort at generalization hazardous. As interest in dogs becomes more specialized, specialized books become available.

New canine medical research brings new remedies almost daily. In the matter of general care it is suggested that a veterinarian be consulted as well as clubs and experienced breeders.

On matters of worming, inoculations and other medical knowledge your veterinarian is your best guide.

Breed clubs are readily available to help with questions on proper mating technique, whelping information, weaning technique, housebreaking technique, and special problems which concern the Saint Bernard.

The recommended reading list below should bring about a wide knowledge of the canine in general and the Saint Bernard specifically:

Anatomy of The Domestic Animals, 4th Edition, Sisson-Grossman, W. B. Saunders Company, Philadelphia, Pa.
Companion Dog Training, Hans Tossutti, Howell Book House Inc.
The Dog in Action, McDowell Lyon, Howell Book House Inc.
Fact and Fiction About Our Breed, Arthur Hesser, The Saint Bernard Club of America, Inc.
Guide to the Dissection of the Dog, Malcolm E. Miller, 3rd Edition, Edwards Brothers, Inc., Ann Arbor, Michigan.
Housebreaking and Feeding Puppies, Edith Creutz Kelly, Howell Book House Inc.
How to Breed Dogs, 2nd Edition, Howell Book House Inc.
How to Trim, Groom and Show Your Dog, Blanche Saunders, Howell Book House Inc.
The New Art of Breeding Better Dogs, Philip Onstott, Howell Book House Inc.
The New Knowledge of Dog Behavior, Clarence Pfaffenberger, Howell Book House Inc.
The Physiology of Domestic Animals, 7th Edition, H. H. Dukes, Comstock Publishing Associates, Ithaca, New York
The Saint Bernard Standard, American Kennel Club

DANNY VON REGENSBERG, brought from the Sauliamt Kennels in Zurich by Edward Poor, secretary of the SBCA, stands in the Acton, Mass. snow.

Interpretation of the Standard

NOTHING in this chapter is intended as an objection to the official Saint Bernard standard, or an attempt to contradict or revise it. The wording of the standard can be changed only by action of the Saint Bernard Club of America, with approval of the American Kennel Club. The Saint Bernard Club of Switzerland would also be consulted.

The purpose of any breed standard is an attempt, and in no case can it be more than an attempt, to define perfection, in order to determine how fine or how faulty may be the dogs under consideration.

No apology need be made for offering an explanation of the written standard. Any document prepared by men, then read by other men, is subject to interpretation. This is why the Supreme Court of the United States sometimes reaches decisions by a vote of five to four.

The beginning fancier in any breed frequently asks why there seems to be no way by which all dogs within that breed can be precisely evaluated. Since this chapter is addressed to beginners and not to experts, its first goal will be to answer that question.

OUTLINE CHART OF A STANDARD-TYPE SAINT BERNARD

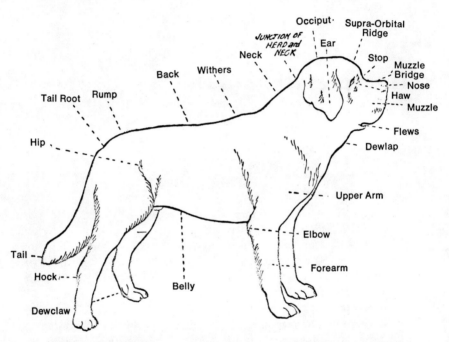

This drawing shows the anatomical parts of the dog as commonly used in descriptions and criticism of points.

The beginner frequently charges that the language of his breed standard is obscure. The second goal of this chapter will be to explain the reasons for that obscurity.

The third goal will be, not to revise, but to explain portions of the Saint Bernard standard in ways which may seem less obscure to the beginner.

The fourth goal will be to add some material not covered in the standard at all, in the hope of clarifying in the mind of the beginner what constitutes a good Saint Bernard.

General Analysis

The language of any breed standard is more or less anthropomorphic, that is, the dogs are described in the same phrases which man uses to describe himself. This is flattering to dogs. The better man likes an animal, the more man-like become the phrases used to describe that animal.

Man finds it impossible to achieve perfection in himself. Assuming that the improbable goal of controlling every word and action could be achieved, perfection still can not be reached because society's definition of perfection includes many contradictions. A man is required to be at once aggressive and reserved, dignified and gay, possessed of initiative and patience.

Realizing the impossibility of human rightness, man hopes that his dog can achieve within canine limitations a degree of perfection which he himself cannot reach. This is why people have dogs.

When man attempts to describe perfection in his chosen breed of dog, he invariably transfers his own contradictions. He demands that the dog be aggressive and gentle, sturdy and graceful, friendly and firm. Man insists that his dog distinguish instantly between burglar and milkman, which is more than he can do himself. Man wants a dog that never starts a dog fight, but never loses one either.

The surprising thing is that many dogs do approach success in meeting the compromises demanded of them.

With all dogs called on in some degree to carry this anthropomorphic burden, the Saint Bernard quite possibly carries the greatest burden of all, because man's approach to the Saint is closely linked to himself.

There are many reasons for this. The immediately obvious reason

141

is that the Saint Bernard, among all breeds of dogs, has a forehead most closely resembling that of man. Admired along with the noble brow is the square jaw, the two together indicating, in man's own terms, the admired combination of intelligence and determination. Add to this the fact that the Saint Bernard is impressively big and impressively strong, yet his strength is in most cases easy to discipline and control. These are attributes sought in both guardian and servant.

Beyond all this, the Saint enjoys a well deserved reputation for life saving, to which task he applies intelligence and vigor plus sensory acuity beyond that of man. Putting life saving to one side, the Saint's status as a working dog is based on his use as a draft animal, to which task he applies docility, strength, and endurance. Being an effective guardian for small children, the Saint can, at the end of his day's work, fill in as your baby-sitter for the evening.

The intention here is not to establish that the Saint Bernard is the "finest dog of all." Since the preference for any one breed is entirely subjective, such a contention would give rise to endless and futile argument.

The intention is to point out that it is perhaps more difficult than with any other breed to avoid describing the Saint Bernard in terms of attributes which we like to believe are "human." In this respect, based on appearance if for no other reason, the Saint is the "ultimate dog."

This increases the difficulty of clarifying a breed standard. How can we clearly describe a dog who resembles a human being when we can't decide what a human being should be like?

Functional Analysis

The problem can be approached in terms of function. The Saint Bernard is a working dog, and the function of his body is to pull. In any evaluation of his body, it must be remembered that anything which contributes to his pulling ability is good; anything which detracts from it is not good.

The body of a good Saint Bernard bears a functional resemblance to the body of a good Percheron or Belgian horse, in that it looks able to pull. The requirements for straight and heavy-boned front legs, heavy-muscled and angulated back legs, in-line leg action, symmetrically massive and close-coupled legs and body, are all part of

142

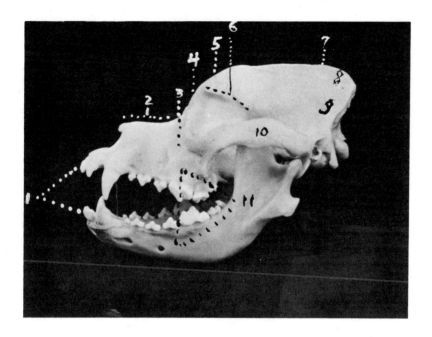

KEY

1. Teeth (lower and upper mandibles)
2. Muzzle bridge
3. Muzzle root
4. Stop
5. Frontal crest
6. Supraorbital process

7. Temporal line
8. Exterior occipital protuberance (Occiput)
9. Exterior occipital crest
10. Zygomatic system (arch)
11. Mandibles (upper half and lower half)

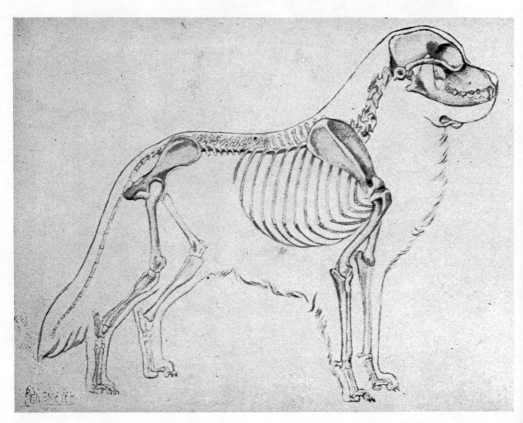

Skeleton Diagram and External Outline of Standard Type St. Bernard Dog.

144

Сн. Stoan's Beau-Zeau, C.D.X. pulls 1000 pounds for first place in a local sled-dog club near Kent, Washington. "Bozo" later pulled 1600 pounds. The enormous power of the dog as he pulls and pushes can be felt just looking at the photograph. "Bozo" is owned by Mr. Stanley A. Zielinski, Jr.

the specification which a mechanical engineer would write if he were asked to design a four-legged animal which could pull.

The head of a Saint Bernard has a different function, in this case entirely subjective. Having insisted that the good Saint be wise, gentle, kindly, determined, capable, and fearless, we expect him to look the part. The official standard attempts with considerable success to describe this anthropomorphic evaluation in terms of lines and measurements. We also insist, however, that the good Saint be "handsome." No description of parts can possibly define handsomeness, but we look for it all the same.

A third function of the Saint Bernard, this time for the satisfaction of his owners, is that he be recognizable as such. Because of the wide publicity which the breed has enjoyed, and because of his size and his very distinctive head markings, the Saint would probably win an identification contest conducted among non-fanciers.

145

The official standard is tolerant of variations in color and markings. By its omissions, it implies that handsomeness in a Saint may be reached in many different ways. To be recognized by a non-fancier, the Saint need be marked only in some combination of brown (meaning anything from orange through red to near-black) and white, with the absolute minimum of brown being the two ears, and the absolute minimum of white being the nose (hopefully with a trace of blaze), chest, four feet, and tip of tail. The point to describing these limits, broad as they are, is that outside them, the non-fancier is entitled to ask what kind of a dog it is.

The range of allowed markings is probably as great as that of any other breed standard, with the principal concern being a recognizable head. Beyond that, the emphasis lies essentially on soundness and strength.

Again by its omissions, the Saint Bernard standard shares with many other breeds an attempt to get away from the idea that there is a difference between a "show dog" and a "pet." To be sure, dog showing is a sport, and in any sport there is a tendency for the rules to become esoteric, but the strong, healthy, and good-natured pet of whom we can justifiably be proud will do his share of winning.

The show-winning Saint Bernard and the really fine working pet Saint Bernard are one and the same. Both the judge and the owner want the Saint to look pleasant enough to welcome a guest, big enough to scare off a burglar, strong enough to pull a wagon, smart enough to rescue a drowning man, and patient enough to look after the children.

Specific Analysis

Breed standards are for the most part written by committees and modified by other committees, which fact tends to reduce the personal element but also tends to reduce clarity. The Saint Bernard standard, furthermore, is a direct translation from that adopted in 1887 at a congress in Zurich, Switzerland.

Any translator, no matter how skilled, has the problem of deciding between literal and conceptual accuracy. The presently approved translation, published in 1959 by the Saint Bernard Club of America, is reprinted in the next chapter.

In preparing, for the benefit of the beginner, a specific clarifica-

CH. BEAU CHEVAL AS EVER ROMA SUMIT
Bred, born, reared and shown in America, this rough coated bitch is decidedly feminine when compared with the more massive-headed male.

International **CH. HERTA v. HUTTWIL**
Bred, born, reared and shown in Europe, this rough coated bitch is an amazing look alike to the above female. Her head type is feminine yet typical. The freckles on her muzzle are a fault and unusual on a European Saint. However overall quality makes up for one deviation.

147

Saint Bernards enjoy pulling carts and sleds. Occasionally, they enjoy pulling each other. Maverick, a perfect gentleman, gives the lovely lady Saint, Paris, a ride around the property of their owners, Mr. and Mrs. Joseph Raap. Both above Saints are rough coated.

Below, "Liebchin" agrees with the standard that "smooths" should have equal *everything* when compared with the roughs. Owners: Mr. and Mrs. Lounsbury.

tion of the standard, the editors have attempted to consult every Saint Bernard specialty judge in North America. Feeling, however, that the words of one man are inevitably clearer than the words of a committee, the editors present here without change a statement from Henry E. Wedig, Sr., M.D., of Cincinnati, Ohio. Dr. Wedig writes:

"Head structure is of prime importance as principal feature of breed identification. The skull should be massive, and the jaws equipped with teeth that are of even bite and strong development. The head must be wide, slightly arched, with the sides sloping gently into a curve that blends with strongly developed cheek bones. The occiput is only moderately developed. The supraorbital ridge is very strongly developed and forms nearly a right angle with the horizontal axis of the head.

"Deeply imbedded between the eyes and starting at the root of the muzzle, a furrow runs over the whole skull, strongly marked at the front section, and gradually disappearing at the base of the occiput. The lines at the sides of the head diverge from the outer corner of the eyes toward the back of the head. The skin of the forehead, above the eyes, forms rather noticeable wrinkles, more or less pronounced, which converge toward the furrow. When the dog is in action, these wrinkles are more prominent, without in the least giving the impression of morosity. These wrinkles must not be too strongly developed. (For definition of parts, see "Outline Chart"— Ed.)

"The slope of the skull to the muzzle is abrupt and rather steep. The muzzle is short, does not taper, and the vertical depth at the root of the muzzle must be greater than the length of the muzzle. The muzzle bridge is straight in most instances; however, a slight break in this straight line is not seriously objectionable. A wide, well-marked shallow furrow runs from the root of the muzzle over the entire bridge to the nose.

"The flews of the upper jaw are strongly developed, and not sharply cut, but turning into a beautiful curve into the lower edge and slightly overhanging. The flews of the lower jaw must not be too pendant. The nose is very substantial, broad with wide open nostrils, and like the lips, always black.

"The ears are of medium size, rather high set, with a very strongly developed burr at the base. They stand slightly away from the head at the base, then drop with a sharp bend to the side and cling to the head without a turn. The flap is tender and forms a rounded triangle, slightly elongated toward the point, with the front edge lying firmly to the head, whereas the back edge stands away from the head somewhat, especially when the dog is at attention. A strongly developed ear gives the skull a squarer, broader and more impressive appearance. (Dr. Wedig's excellent description of the ears neglects to mention that the ears, even more than the eyes, are the Saint Bernard's most expressive feature. In action and at attention, the Saint's ears are frequently though subtly changing their position.—Ed.)

"The eyes are set to the front, and are of medium size, dark brown, with intelligent, friendly expression, and set moderately deep. The lower eyelids, as a rule, do not close completely, and in these cases there is an angular wrinkle toward the inner corner of the eye. Eyelids must not be too pendant, or show a deep red haw.

"The neck is set high and is very strong. It must fully support the head in all angles of position and usage, and fully coordinate the muscular movements of the shoulders and foreback section, into which the neck blends.

"The back is strong, very broad, and straight as far as the haunches; from there gently sloping to the rump. A gentle, almost imperceptible merger into the root of the tail is mandatory. Strong, well developed chest structure is important, with a belly drawn up reasonably tight, and well set off from the loin section. The rib cage must be well developed for ample bellows action, but never to the point of being barrel chested.

"Front legs are to be very powerful, with forearms well developed muscularly, and are to be straight and strong. Legs should be sufficiently long to give a good working stride, with reasonable daylight underneath the dog, but without creating an impression of undue legginess. The shoulder is well muscled and placed in close apposition to the forward trunk section, with the shoulder blade ridge being well angulated in relation to the arms of the front leg.

"The hindquarters must be very strong, with impressively muscular legs, and there must be moderate angulation of the hocks. Dewclaws are permissible, so long as they do not interfere with the gait. Feet must be broad with strong toes, moderately closed, with rather high knuckles.

CH. SANCTUARY WOODS GOING MY WAY, Smooth male, owned by Mr. and Mrs. Alvin Holt. "Going" won the honor of Best of Breed at the 1970 Saint Bernard Club of America Specialty show held near Concord, California.
Sire: Ch. Sanctuary Woods You Lucky Boy
Dam: Ch. Sanctuary Woods Vanity

"Most important of all, there must be a well synchronized application of power transmission from the pads of the feet throughout the entire leg structure, fore and aft, to the muscles of the back and shoulders. This could be designated as the 'power drive factor,' and is a fundamental must for all properly constructed dogs. All dogs so possessed are able to move with a good springing step and a back movement that is completely smooth and free.

"The tail starts broad and powerful directly from the rump and is long, very heavy, ending in a powerful tip. In repose it hangs straight down, bending in the lower third only, with a slight turn to the side permissible. In action the tail is carried at or slightly above the level position, but may not be erect or rolled over the back.

"There are rough and smooth coated Saint Bernards; both have identical body structure. Judges are to consider them of equal value. Any of the several distinguishing features between rough and smooth Saint Bernards must be considered a matter of personal choice as to which one may prefer to own.

"Body weights may vary greatly and are not taken into account in judging, except that it is considered favorable for a dog to be in good flesh, carrying its best weight, without the slightest suggestion of obesity.

"The official breed standard has been used extensively in composing this presentation. My own ideas have been interwoven as well, to amplify those points I have considered important beyond the scope of the standard.

"It would be entirely possible for any Saint Bernard owner to study the breed standard, to read over the various breed publications, to attend dog shows and evaluation events; and I am certain that it would be possible for that owner to evaluate his own stock as well as any of the licensed judges, providing that he is able to approach his task with an open mind, using the simple facts alone, and able to recognize the failings that may be present in the dog being evaluated. This need not in any sense detract from the value we place on the dog in terms of personal warmth and affection, which most of us have for these dogs that so easily become a part of our lives and our homes."

With the end of the quotation from Dr. Wedig, the editors are grateful to him for his analysis, in which he adheres to the standard in his capacity as a specialty judge, clarifies it in his capacity as a

CH. WILHELMINA OF SHAGG-BARK
Owned by Mr. and Mrs. James Crook

CH. SERENDIPITY'S OCTAVIUS
Owned and bred by Judith Goldworm
Judge: Fred Andersen
Handler: Ray Curry

American and Canadian CH.
THE BLUE CHIP OF CANTERBURY
Breeder: James Crook
Owner: Betty Roberts
Handler: Don Hoglund
Judge: Clyde Smith

This head study of "Titan" helps one understand why he is called one of the most typical Saints of contemporary time.

Too often at ringside we forget the playful side of the mighty show dog. Here is a rare photo of the famous CH. TITAN VON MALLEN at play at home in New Jersey.

"Titan" with his owner, Mr. Louis Mallen, practices for a show which will, no doubt, bring more fame.

CH. FALCONRIDGE ST. ELMO
frolics with his mistress, June W. Shew. This fine, rough-coated male was whelped
October 17, 1964.

medical practitioner, and demonstrates warm affection in his capacity as a lover of Saint Bernards.

Additional Analysis

The standard states in Paragraph 6 that "the neck in action is carried erect," a phrase which probably has suffered in translation of the words "in action." When posed or at attention, the Saint Bernard carries his head high, with his head and neck posture creating the impression that he is quite able to hold his own head up, without assistance, perhaps in order to get a better view.

When running free, without pulling, the head and neck are held approximately level, or raised slightly if a view of the ground ahead is required. When at work pulling a load, the Saint's head drops in proportion to his work effort, in exactly the same manner as a draft horse's head drops in order to get a better mechanical purchase on his load. When tracking, the Saint's head will fit the need, that is, raised for wind testing, then lowered for ground tracking.

The standard is silent on the subject of gait. To fill this gap, Dr. Wedig has supplied the phrase "power drive factor," and asks for "a good springing step."

On this point many members of the Saint Bernard fancy have expressed themselves. They wish to correct the often expressed notion that Saints, because strong and heavy, must therefore move ponderously and slowly. The fact is that a good Saint Bernard suits his gait to the occasion. If he is pulling, he digs in, straight and hard. In contrast, when running free the task of carrying himself is so easy he barely seems to touch the ground. The impression of light-footedness and of generally easy movement is very much to be desired.

Left to his own devices, the Saint will adjust the speed of his movement to the situation. If he has only a little way to go, he will walk. If a little farther, he will run slowly. In a playful mood, he gallops. If in his mind an emergency has arisen, he can turn on as great a burst of speed as any racing dog.

Saint Bernard showmen complain that their dogs in competition are frequently assigned to small rings, under the impression that the Saint is a slow mover and therefore doesn't have to go very far. The fallacy here is that the good Saint by nature adjusts his gait to the

MARK TRAIL'S "ANDY"

distance he has to go. He can hardly be persuaded to move freely in a ring six times his own length, and somewhat smaller than his living room at home.

Freedom and ease of motion are as important to a Saint Bernard as to any other dog. The purpose of running is to get from here to there with a maximum of efficiency and a minimum of effort. The gait of a draft animal, however, will be different from that of a pure runner. It has been made clear that the draft animal's legs are most efficient when pulling straight into the load. When this same straight line action is accelerated, the animal's body, because of the necessary width between his legs, will roll slightly. The effect can be clearly observed when a good draft horse is asked to move rapidly. Excessive roll is undesirable, as indicating looseness, but no roll at all in a draft animal indicates too little freedom of movement.

Recent Developments

Many Saint Bernard admirers, perhaps speaking from childhood memories, are fond of saying that Saints are not as big as they used to be. As a matter of fact, they are bigger. The desired shoulder height called for in the standard, of twenty-seven plus inches in the male and twenty-five plus inches in the female, would now be regarded as very small. On the other hand, breeders no longer work toward pure size or weight as ends in themselves.

Even though the average Saint is bigger than he used to be, there is a strong tendency to de-emphasize the importance of size in favor of good proportion, soundness, and freedom of movement. Having achieved pure size and strength, Saint Bernard breeders are now working toward the whole dog, an animal who is not only handsome in all his parts, but completely handsome in the entirety.

The Saint in Pictured Motion

In conveying impressions of motion, the interpretation of a graphic artist is often more effective than photography. The editors close this chapter with a page of action sketches by Ed Dodd, author and artist of the nature serial strip "Mark Trail," whose Saint Bernard, "Andy," is one of the principal characters in the narrative, and thus easily the most widely seen and known Saint on this continent.

159

Mr. Dodd writes, "I honestly believe people are as much concerned with Andy's welfare as they are with Mark Trail's." He adds that the original Andy, real-life model for these sketches, was nine years old when these sketches were done.

The group of sketches, printed here through the courtesy of Mr. Dodd and the Hall Syndicate, Inc., shows Andy in action, readiness for action, and attentive repose. Not only are the sketches correct on all details of movement, but they succeed in conveying the impression of strong and fluid grace which is characteristic of the well-constructed Saint Bernard.

Official Standard of the St. Bernard

As adopted by the Saint Bernard Club of Amer-ica and approved by the American Kennel Club May 12, 1959

Short Haired

GENERAL

Powerful, proportionately tall figure, strong and muscular in every part, with powerful head and most intelligent expression. In dogs with a dark mask the expression appears more stern, but never ill-natured.

HEAD

Like the whole body, very powerful and imposing. The massive skull is wide, slightly arched and the sides slope in a gentle curve into the very strongly developed, high cheek bones. Occiput only moderately developed.

The supra-orbital ridge is very strongly developed and forms nearly a right angle with the horizontal axis of the head.

161

Deeply imbedded between the eyes and starting at the root of the muzzle, a furrow runs over the whole skull. It is strongly marked in the first half, gradually disappearing toward the base of the occiput. The lines at the sides of the head diverge considerably from the outer corner of the eyes toward the back of the head.

The skin of the forehead, above the eyes, forms rather noticeable wrinkles, more or less pronounced, which converge toward the furrow. Especially when the dog is in action, the wrinkles are more visible without in the least giving the impression of morosity. Too strongly developed wrinkles are not desired.

The slope from the skull to the muzzle is sudden and rather steep.

The muzzle is short, does not taper, and the vertical depth at the root of the muzzle must be greater than the length of the muzzle.

The bridge of the muzzle is not arched, but straight; in some dogs, occasionally, slightly broken.

A rather wide, well-marked, shallow furrow runs from the root of the muzzle over the entire bridge of the muzzle to the nose.

The flews of the upper jaw are strongly developed, not sharply cut, but turning in a beautiful curve into the lower edge, and slightly overhanging.

The flews of the lower jaw must not be deeply pendant.

The teeth should be sound and strong and should meet in either a scissors or an even bite; the scissors bite being preferable. The undershot bite, although sometimes found with good specimens, is not desirable. The overshot bite is a fault.

A black roof of the mouth is desirable.

NOSE

The nose (Schwamm)—very substantial, broad, with wide open nostrils, and, like the lips, always black.

EARS

Ears—of medium size, rather high set, with very strongly developed burr (Muschel) at the base. They stand slightly away from the head at the base, then drop with a sharp bend to the side and cling to the head without a turn. The flap is tender and forms a rounded triangle, slightly elongated toward the point, the front edge lying firmly to the head whereas the back edge may stand somewhat away from the head, especially when the dog is at attention. Lightly set ears, which at the base immediately cling to the head, give it an oval and too little marked exterior, whereas a strongly developed base gives the skull a squarer, broader and much more impressive appearance.

EYES

The eyes are set more to the front than the sides, are of medium size, dark brown, with intelligent, friendly expression, set moderately deep. The lower eyelids, as a rule, do not close completely and, if that is the case, form an angular wrinkle toward the inner corner of the eye. Eyelids which are too deeply pendant and show conspicuously the lachrymal glands, or a very red, thick haw, and eyes that are too light, are objectionable.

NECK

The neck is set high, very strong and in action is carried erect, otherwise horizontally or slightly downward. The junction of head and neck is distinctly marked by an indentation. The nape of the neck is very muscular and rounded at the sides which makes the neck appear rather short. The dewlap of throat and neck is well pronounced; too strong development, however, is not desirable.

SHOULDERS

The shoulders are sloping and broad, very muscular and powerful. The withers are strongly pronounced.

CHEST

The chest is very well arched, moderately deep, not reaching below the elbows.

BACK

Very broad, perfectly straight as far as the haunches, from there gently sloping to the rump, and merging imperceptibly into the root of the tail.

HINDQUARTERS

Well developed. Legs very muscular.

BELLY

Distinctly set off from the powerful loin section, only little drawn up.

TAIL

The tail starting broad and powerful directly from the rump is long, very heavy, ending in a powerful tip. In repose it hangs straight down, turning gently upward in the lower third only, which is not to be considered a fault. In a great many specimens the tail is carried with the end slightly bent and therefore hangs down in the shape of an f. In action all dogs carry the tail more or less turned upward. However it may not be carried too erect or by any means rolled over the back. A slight curling of the tip is sooner admissible.

FOREARM

Very powerful and extraordinarily muscular.

FORELEGS

Straight, strong.

HINDLEGS

Hocks of moderate angulation. Dewclaws are not desired; if present they must not obstruct gait.

FEET

Broad, with strong toes, moderately closed, and with rather high knuckles. The so-called dewclaws which sometimes occur on the inside of the hindlegs are imperfectly developed toes. They are of no use to the dog and are not to be taken into consideration in judging. They may be removed by surgery.

COAT

The coat is very dense, short haired (stockhaarig), lying smooth, tough, without however feeling rough to the touch. The thighs are slightly bushy. The tail at the root has longer and denser hair which gradually becomes shorter toward the tip. The tail appears bushy, not forming a flag.

COLOR

White with red or red with white, the red in its various shades; brindle patches with white markings. The colors red and brown-yellow are of entirely equal value. Necessary markings are: white chest, feet and tip of tail, nose band, collar or spot on the nape; the latter and blaze are very desirable. Never of one color or without white. Faulty are all other colors except the favorite dark shadings on the head (mask) and ears. One distinguishes between mantle dogs and splash-coated dogs.

HEIGHT AT SHOULDER

Height at the shoulder of the dog ought to be 27½ inches minimum, of the bitch, 25½ inches. Female animals are of a finer and more delicate build.

FAULTS

Considered as faults are all deviations from the standard, as for instance a sway-back and a disproportionately long back, hocks too much bent, straight hindquarters, upward growing hair in spaces between the toes, out at elbows, cowhocks and weak pasterns.

Long Haired

The long haired type completely resembles the short haired type except for the coat which is not short-haired (stockhaarig) but of medium length, plain to slightly wavy, never rolled or curly and not shaggy either. Usually, on the back, especially in the region of the haunches to the rump, the hair is more wavy, a condition, by the way, that is slightly indicated in the short haired dogs.

The tail is bushy with dense hair of moderate length. Rolled or curly hair on the tail is not desirable. A tail with parted hair, or a flag tail, is faulty. Face and ears are covered with short and soft hair; longer, silky hair at the base of the ear is permissible. Forelegs only slightly feathered, thighs very bushy.

The spiritual communion between the mighty Saint Bernard and children is what has brought so many of these noble animals into thousands of homes all over the world. Here, CH. SUBIRA'S FREDERICK and his friend, are, communicating.

Special Problems of Giant Dogs

by Joe Stetson

A GIANT dog is one which is larger than nature meant the canine species to be. Man's stress on size in the selective breeding program which developed and typed the Saint Bernard breed, as well as other breeds almost as large, has resulted in the production of giants with the glandular characteristics of giantism or acromegaly. These by-products of the sought-after size were certainly not planned by the designers of the breed, but their manifestations must be recognized, and, if desirable dogs are to result, intelligent steps taken in the right direction.

The most important problem of the giant results from the dying of nerve cells in the anterior lobe of the lumbar region of the spine causing breaks in the nerve paths that stimulate muscle patterns in the hindquarters. This is called the "lethal neurone." The muscle patterns thereby unused, atrophy, and the dog is debilitated in accordance with which and how many of the cells die. Subsequent

167

CH. BEAU CHEVAL'S TRACI LA MARDOUG, Smooth bitch, owned and bred by Marlene J. Anderson of Wycombe, Pa. "Traci" won the honor of Best of Opposite Sex to Best of Breed during the 1970 Saint Bernard Club of America Specialty Show held near Concord, California.

Sire: Ch. Powells Magus Von Echo   Dam: Beau Cheval's Showgirl

movement depends upon the remaining muscle patterns and the methods of locomotion substituted for normal gait by the dog, perhaps with the aid of exercise.

This phenomenon occurs in puppyhood and is usually observed at between six and twelve months of age. With no intention of libeling a fine breed, it may be readily observed in some Great Danes, where normal canine locomotion has been replaced by various substitutes, including straight stifled "high behinds," roached backs, dropped croups, or "hinge backs." Bulldogs, occasionally Bassets, Newfoundlands, and, of late years, Irish Wolfhounds demonstrate this characteristic. Improper hindquarter movement has long been a problem with the giant Saint Bernard.

In the last decade Newfoundland breeders have made great strides in eliminating this unsoundness from what they consider their superior individuals. More recently, Saint Bernards are improving in soundness, a trend which should become a mandate with the fancy. How is the problem solved? By considering soundness over size in judging and in selecting individuals for breeding. More than this; refuse to show or use for breeding any specimen, no matter how grand the size or head if it is a victim of the "lethal neurone." Recognize the limits nature has placed upon the species and respect them.

Lazy whelping is another problem confronting owners and breeders of dogs with the glandular idiosyncrasies of the giant. At birth puppies of average-sized dogs weigh from one-twenty-fifth to one-fiftieth the weight of the dam. Toy pups may be as large as one-twentieth. Despite the fact that Saint puppies rarely weigh more than one one-hundredth the weight of their mother, and therefore whelping should involve no mechanical difficulty, one or more pups may not be whelped. Should this occur, septicemia is likely to result. Care must be taken to assure the expelling of all puppies and preferably on schedule. X-ray can be used if a careful temperature check on the bitch has warned of trouble. In the meantime the veterinarian can administer drugs to stimulate whelping.

Intestinal torsion is another problem of the giant dog. When stoppages occur with resulting bloat, time is of the essence in arresting the formation of gases and thus reducing the pressure, which may cause rupture of the stomach or intestines or death by pressure on the heart. Anti-ferments may be used and the veterinarian may find

169

it necessary to tap the inflated area as is done to a horse suffering from colic.

Glandular imbalance in giants is probably also responsible for the irregular seasons and low percentage of conception which some breeders observe in their kennels.

There is some possibility that the quality of bone found in the giants may contribute to occurrence of rickets, a subject usually thought of only in terms of feeding. Some large, well-fed puppies develop bone poorly, while more nearly average-sized pups, even when poorly fed for perhaps economic reasons, are straight boned.

Some specimens of the giant breeds exhibit short life spans, with proneness to diabetes, heart conditions, and more than average distress from arthritis. This is yet another result of pushing the size factor beyond what was naturally evolved as the canine species.

These warnings do not, however, mean that size is in itself bad. All of these problems can be solved by not pushing nature's formula too far.

By virtue of their very size, Saint Bernards present other special problems not particularly medical in nature. For one thing, large dogs are just too big physically to breed small virgin bitches. The solution to this problem is either artificial insemination, which has as yet a rather low percentage of success, or using the larger stud only after breeding to one more nearly the bitch's size.

Anal glands require the periodic pressure of normal stools in order to function properly. It is often difficult to establish economically practical diets which maintain firm stools in large breeds. Anything less than a firm stool allows the contents of the anal glands to accumulate. When this condition becomes extreme, inflammation, tissue damage and infection ensue. Every practical means to maintain stools of adequate consistency is indicated, in lieu of which periodic manual pressure on the anal glands to approximate their normal secretion will avoid trouble.

The skin and coat covering the joints upon which large dogs must lie are often subject to harsh use, since Saints prefer to lie on cool concrete or stone surfaces, especially in warm weather. The heaviest coated dog can wear his coat thin on the elbows, hocks, and breastbone. When the skin becomes so calloused as to block the hair follicles, accumulation of fluid or infection sometimes follows. At best the calloused areas are unpleasing in appearance. One solution is to

Rebecca and Barbara Montross, twin daughters of Mr. and Mrs. Harold Montross, Madison, Wisconsin, sit among armloads of potential love.

KESSOPULOS'S AUGUSTUS CAESAR, U.D. goes through the arduous exercises required in order to qualify for the Utility Dog obedience degree. "Caesar" clearly proves the Saint Bernard to be highly intelligent, agile and powerful.

172

CH. DOWN'S SNOW ANGEL,
C.D. verifies that a lady
Saint is equally gifted in
the areas of intellect, agil-
ity, strength and beauty.

make a summer pad covered with oilcloth, plastic or other cool material and encourage the dog to use it. Should callouses develop, keep them lubricated with a light, clear oil.

The mechanics of breeding large dogs, where proportionate differences between the sexes are considerable and the dogs are too heavy to assist, can be aided by the preparation of a breeding platform. This consists of a number of boards covered with matting, which can be arranged as the circumstances require.

When not left free to take care of themselves, the large and especially the heavy-coated dogs are subject to heat exhaustion. Reasonable anticipation can prevent this by never confining a dog in automobile, room, or other sun exposure that can bring him to grief. If the accident occurs, however, the quickest way to reduce body temperature is to apply cool, wet compresses to the belly. Should cool water not be available, use cool metal or any good heat conductor at hand in order to draw heat from the large blood vessels lying close to the surface. Ice cubes wrapped in a cloth may save the day, but the best advice is not to leave your big dog in a closed car in the first place.

Hip dysplasia is a subject which continues to be controversial as to cause and possible prevention or remedy. We do know that dogs which are well developed muscularly and get plenty of exercise are rarely disturbed by it. There are many examples of dogs which have been apparently normal, then later lost their sockets when softened by lives of comfort and ease with new masters. Considering the size of Saint Bernards and their rapid growth rate, which competes with exercise in the growing period of large breeds, every effort should be made to keep them in hard condition for their well being in general and the condition of their hip sockets in particular.

The Growth Pattern of a Giant Dog

In the growth pattern of a puppy intended by nature to gain eighty to a hundred pounds in the first six months of his life, every day is important. It is not sufficient to say that because the puppy is apparently healthy and well nourished, he will get along all right. During his period of rapid growth, the giant puppy develops different parts at different times. Tomorrow morning he will not even look the same as he did the night before. Therefore a health deficiency lasting only a few days in a giant puppy can leave a deficiency or impairment in the grown dog.

One of the requirements imposed upon the owner of a giant puppy is continuous attention to his health problems. The puppy is growing so fast in so many different places that a week of ill health can be disastrous to the perfection of his eventual development.

Scientific progress continuously improves techniques for the benefit of man and dog. At this writing, however, there are well developed means at hand for immunizing a high percentage of dogs against distemper, infectious hepatitis, rabies and leptospirosis. When used with care, these methods have proved successful. It may be surmised that these methods, though they may be slightly modified, will not be outmoded for years to come.

We now know that puppies normally acquire a blood level of antibodies from their mother both prenatally and by way of the colostrum in the milk of early nursing. This level is roughly dependent upon the mother's own antibody level and tapers off until, in puppies of a well immunized mother, it approaches insufficient protection from exposure to distemper and infectious hepatitis at from six to twelve weeks.

To afford maximum protection an injection of permanent vaccine at six weeks should be given. If antibody level is low enough for a puppy to be vulnerable at this time, the vaccine will be a challenge and immunity will be established. If the antibody level is high, the antibodies will prevent the modified virus in the vaccine from challenging successfully and no additional immunity will be produced. Such initially better protected puppies must then be vaccinated again at twelve weeks when the level of immunity is low enough for the vaccine to challenge successfully.

From this description it is obvious that one of the vaccinations will be wasted. Only one is necessary to give protection providing it is given at twelve weeks of age or later. This schedule can be used if it is considered safe to leave the puppies vulnerable until they are three months old. In this respect the location of the kennel, exposure to street virus, high level of immunity of the mother, and general health factors should be considered.

Such considerations should also affect the decision on whether or not to use serum in an immunizing program for a puppy. Serum can offer only very temporary protection, and yet permanent vaccine can not be administered successfully until the serum has become ineffective. In any case there must be a period of vulnerability before the vaccine can constitute a challenge. Granted a reasonable degree of protection from infection, many veterinarians have abandoned the use of serum in favor of permanent vaccine.

Leptospirosis and rabies, transferred by the urine and saliva, respectively, of infected animals, need not be guarded against where puppies are concerned until a later time when they may be exposed. Leptospirosis protection, when later required, must presently be periodically repeated. Modified-live-virus rabies vaccine provides lifetime immunity.

Body temperature, whether in a giant puppy or a grown dog, is the best indication of good health. The normal rectal temperature of a dog is 101.5 to 102 degrees Fahrenheit, with the higher limit more likely after meals, at the end of the day, or during excitement. A degree or more below or above the normal bracket is reason for concern and careful observation.

175

Then, back to the joy of working with the master. In this series MARDONOF'S BRUNNEHILDA V. WORY, C.D., owned by Mr. and Mrs. H. Cropsey, Kailua, Oahu, Hawaii, does obedience work. Above, "Hilda" powers herself up and over the bar hurdle. She brings her front legs up immediately.

As her front clears the high jump her front legs reach forward in preparation to land, but her hindquarters will stay close to her body until they are clear of the hurdle. One sees beautiful mental, nerve and muscle coordination in motion. "Hilda" jumps 34 inches for practice. In obedience trials she must jump her height at the shoulder which is 32 inches.

Hilda returns over the jump with the dumbell she went to retrieve. This very complicated obedience exercise does not find Hilda lacking.

Hilda flies over the difficult broad jump. She does not curl her legs under her for this exercise as there is no need. She must gain enough height so that when she lands her hind legs clear the front board. The enormous drive of her rear quarters makes this duck soup for her.

Credit: The editors thank Mr. and Mrs. Cropsey for this series and, especially, Mrs. Rex Roberts who offered them for this edition.

Shafer photo

At the 1963 Westminster Kennel Club show, judge Virgil Johnson awarded CH. HAAGEN VON NARBENHOLT and his younger full brother WUNDERBAR the title of best brace in show. This being an all-time first for Saints at Westminster, the New England St. Bernard Club promptly voted 15-year-old handler Jessica Roberts a lifetime membership.

Schley photo

CH. CAREY'S ACCENT ON FANTABULOUS (Ch. Sanctuary Woods Fantabulous ex Bubbling Over of Four Winds), owned by Susan Carey and bred by John Carey. This rough male is shown winning under George Schroth, handler Cliff Nippress.

In this day of easy transportation, with qualified veterinarians usually available, there are still times when general recommendations can be helpful. A dog with abnormal temperature should be helped to a place where he can be observed and treated. Such a place should be dry, draft free, and reasonably warm. A dog with subnormal temperature, resulting from organic failure, loss of blood, exposure or poisoning, should be kept warm. A dog whose energies are being used to fight an invading disease will also be helped by warmth.

Diets will generally be prescribed in accordance with each situation. Frequent, small feedings are helpful. If the dog must be force fed, a simple method is to prepare food in liquid form and pour it slowly between the lips at one side of the mouth, while holding the dog's lips closed on the other side. The head need be tipped only slightly upward to facilitate swallowing.

One thing to remember in getting a dog to eat of his own initiative is that a dog associates food with scent. He is unlikely to want to eat what he can not smell. Cleaning the nostrils of a sick dog with a mild saline solution will often make the difference. If he can smell a piece of meat he will rarely refuse to eat it.

An attack of distemper suffered by a growing giant dog can seriously affect his later development. The distemper virus may take various forms. The virus is able to attack such tissue as is derived from the epithelium, that is, tissue which covers surfaces, forms glands and lines most cavities of the body, such as the lungs and intestines. When the virus is successfully attacking the lungs, the illness is respiratory, or intestinal when that area is the object of attack. When, usually after weakening the victim by successful invasion of lungs or intestines, the virus attacks the central nervous system, the illness becomes the nervous type, referred to at times as chorea or St. Vitus' Dance.

CH. BETINA VON ROSENBORG, rough-coated bitch, bred and owned by Henry Frederiksen, enjoys the luxury of the indoor life
Sire: Ch. Baron von Hannibal   Dam: Ch. Tessy Queen Von Rosenborg

The nervous type, known as encephalitis, is usually delayed by some resistance to the virus getting through the so-called spinal barrier. When it does attack it destroys the nerve sheaths, leaving them exposed to stimuli. Thus exposed, the muscles which the nerve path would normally cause to contract at the dog's volition are instead contracted spasmodically. When the nerve tissue damage is not too great, the dog often learns to compensate and seems quite normal until, in a period of stress or excitement, he suspends his effort to compensate. Then the uncontrolled stimuli take over and the dog jerks, or has convulsions or running fits. The debility caused by nerve tissue damage may be compensated for by the dog, but never repaired.

Obviously, the best cure for distemper is not to let your dog get it in the first place.

The same thought applies to heartworm, which is not an intestinal worm at all and thus not detectable through feces examination. Heartworm, until recently considered regional, has been spread country-wide as a result of transporting dogs great distances for benching, breeding, hunting, and field trials. A single dog, run or shown in heartworm territory, can return to infest an entire kennel or neighborhood.

Heartworm becomes a detriment to a dog when the adult worms lodge in large blood vessels or the chambers of the heart, reducing circulation efficiency chiefly because of the space they occupy. Once there they can be removed only with great difficulty, through the use of drugs, and some cases may be beyond treatment.

There is a prophylaxis, however, which will prevent adult worms from appearing. Since the microfilariae which become adult heartworms require about a hundred days to do so, quarterly administration of caricide in proper dosage kills the microfilariae and adults never reach the heart. In heartworm territory, this preventive measure has become essential to the success of bird dog activities, in which a debilitated dog is of little value. Any dog with a light infestation of adult worms can be kept from further damage by killing the microfilariae before they mature.

Periodic treatment with caricide for heartworm prevention will also rid the dog of any roundworms he may be carrying. This is especially important when dogs are with children, or defecate where children might make contact. The ingesting of embryonated round-

181

LUX-LINKSMADER, Swiss import Canadian CH. ROCK ISLE HEIDI
The above specimens are owned by Mrs. Betty-Ann Hicks, British Columbia. The similarity between the Swiss-born 9-month-old smooth dog (left) and the Canadian-born smooth bitch (right) shows that correct head type is not any one nation's monopoly

182

worm eggs from either dog or cat, by humans, can cause considerable trouble. Canine roundworms, differing from the human roundworms, become aberrant in human beings. Instead of passing through the intestinal wall into the bloodstream, entering the lungs, being coughed up and swallowed to renew the cycle in the intestines, they circulate in the bloodstream. From there they may lodge in various parts of the body with varying results, including enlargement of the liver, a muscle pain similar to trichina, or a condition in the cornea of the eye which has been mistaken for carcinoma.

Roundworms are often ignored because adult dogs usually seem to tolerate them. A rapidly growing giant puppy, however, is a different story. Puppies can acquire them prenatally and thus be retarded or killed. Roundworms are easily eliminated, and in view of the danger both to puppies and to human beings, there seems no reason why roundworm infestation should be tolerated.

Photo: Courtesy Beaulah von Arnim

Whether large or small, Saint Bernards have an affinity for children even beyond that of many other dogs. Here is a young fancier enjoying the company of two very special friends.

Eighteen champions in one ring. Dog photographer Brown used his panoramic camera to get them all.

184

A Week-End with the Saints

A BROAD look at the Saint Bernard was achieved during the long Memorial Day week-end of 1963. The three-day event, in quality, quantity, and comprehensive breed coverage, has been described as "once-in-a-lifetime." More important, the wide sampling permitted a definitive analysis of the present state of the breed.

The event attracted widespread attention from outside the fancy. Arithmetic-minded historians have discovered many world's records, at least one of which may stand for a long while; an all-time, all-breed record for pounds on the paw. As part of the week-end's program, every participating Saint was weighed-in, registered, and photographed, thus providing broad information on what a well-conditioned Saint Bernard, 1963 style, weighed.

Heaviest dog was Ch. Powell's Triston of Riga, at 217 pounds. He was brought to the scales by the SBCA vice-president, Laurence Powell. A few others, looking equally heavy, were around the two hundred mark.

The weight spread between dogs, all of good quality, was wide. Adult males for the most part ran from 150 through 195. Adult females ranged evenly from 130 through 170, with the complete spread being from 120 to 186.

Mazanec photo

CH. SIEGFRIED VON ALPENHOF was weigh-in number one to begin the week-end. Officials are Charles Sorenson, weighmaster, and Rex Roberts, week-end chairman.

Mazanec photo

A handler class, during Demonstration Day at the 1963 Saint Bernard week-end, pauses to let television photographers get some cheesecake. Embracing owner Al Saba is CH. QUEEN OF SHEBA OF SHADY HOLLOW, top-winning Saint bitch in 1961.

CH. SWITZER OF SHADY HOLLOW, chosen by judge A. Alfred LePine as Best of Breed at the Saint Bernard Club of America specialty. Handler, Jane Forsyth; owner, Phyllis Jackson of North Windham, Conn.

Mr. LePine's choice for Best of Opposite Sex, CH. GERDA CHRISTINA OF SKYCROFT. Handler, William Trainor; owner, Maritta Cox, of Seville, Ohio.

At the New England Saint Bernard Club specialty, judge Dorothy Breyfogle moved Gerda Christina to Best of Breed. Here she faces her full brother, CH. GERO CHRISTOPHER OF SKYCROFT, who was judged Best of Opposite Sex.

CH. KOBI VON STEINERNHOF, whose owner, Charles Cawker, of Foxboro, Ontario, brought him to the United States for the first time, was handled by Jessica Roberts and judged Winners Dog and Best of Winners by both Mr. LePine and Mrs. Breyfogle for a history making ten-point week-end.

The average weight of all Saints which crossed the scales, including dogs, bitches, and puppies over six months, was 153 pounds, or about thirteen dogs to the ton. The accumulated weight of all entries came to just under seventeen tons.

Observation on Type

One conclusion to be drawn from the week-end's showing was that the emphasis on sheer bulk as a criterion of Saint Bernard quality has vanished. While remaining securely in first place with the heaviest of dogs, Saint breeders have abandoned bulk in favor of soundness, condition, and excellence of movement. The typical Saint now seems to have four good legs under him, not just the front two.

A Dedicated Fancy

The Saint Bernard is not a status symbol, he is a member of the family. The station wagons arriving for the week-end contained at least as many children as dogs. The breed is largely owner-trained and handled, with about ninety per cent of the owners handling their own dogs in the ring. No matter what the distance, once entered, the Saint Bernard family shows up. The number of absentees at the week-end was less than one-third that normally expected at a dog show.

Photo by Gundy and Bernie Epting
"Sherpa," BARON DINO VON CRAILSHEIM, is depicted with his mountaineer master on the trail enroute to Mt. Hozameen in British Columbia. "Sherpa" started backpacking at thirteen months of age. Now that he is full grown, he carries 45 pounds on mountaineering expeditions

The Saint Fancier's Forum

IT IS DIFFICULT not to notice a Saint Bernard, therefore owners get accustomed to answering questions. When Saint fanciers get together, they compare notes on how to answer. Here are some of their suggestions.

How Can I Find the Right Puppy?

The person who asks the question should be congratulated, and answered carefully, beginning with the counter-question, "What kind of puppy do you and your children want?" Children and puppies go together, but there are differences. The puppies grow up faster and cost less. In selecting a puppy, you can decide which one you want, rather than take pot-luck.

Any dog, and especially the Saint Bernard, becomes a working member of the family. When you acquire a dog, or a child, you acquire a responsibility and a delight. In either case, you will have to do some work and spend some money.

An average dog, over his average lifetime, will cost you a good deal more than his purchase price, but over the years it's a bargain-

191

CH. EMIR V. WENGIBACH, bred, born, reared and shown in Europe, this Smooth dog is a worthy representative of his continent.

E.H. Frank Photo

CH. SANCTUARY WOODS CYCLONE, bred, born, reared and shown in America, this Smooth dog is a worthy representative of his continent.

As the world grows smaller due to jet travel, the Saint world follows. It is fascinating to compare overall quality, breed type and balance of dogs who have been bred in Europe to dogs bred in America. Americans linebreed; Europeans seldom do. It is eye-opening to see how closely dogs resemble where the only route in common was breeder conception on what a fine Saint should look like.

Twomey Photo
CH. AIMING HI BLIZZARD, (Zwinghof Aiming Hi Dr. Bartolo ex Ch. Sanctuary Woods Regalia) a rough, owned and bred by William C. Cooley, is shown scoring points enroute to his championship under judge Joe Gregory, Mrs. Cooley handling.

basement installment plan with no interest charges, and perhaps twenty times less than the cost of raising an average child. Dogs have to be fed, but at bargain rates. They have to be housed and cared for, but most of them are adaptable and healthy. They need to be educated, but the tuition charge is low.

In any case, you will want to get as much reward as you can for your money. The most important step is to pick the right puppy. Here is how you go about it.

1. Inform yourself about the breed of your choice, which is probably a Saint Bernard, because otherwise you wouldn't be reading this book. There are books about every breed. Buy one, or several, and do your homework.

2. Inform yourself about nearby breeders. A good source of information is reached through breed clubs. Almost every breed has a national club, and area clubs. There may be an expert on your

chosen breed who lives just around the corner. To find him, borrow a dog show catalog from anyone who shows dogs. Any such catalog will list dogs from a hundred or more different breeds, and the names and addresses of their owners. Select the name of the nearest owner and ask him for the name and address of the area club's secretary. Then ask the secretary for the names of the nearest breeders.

3. Attend a meeting of the breed club in your area, or better still, join the club. This is a quick way of getting acquainted with people who know more about the breed than you do. You'll also meet some good dogs. For further acquaintance, go to a dog show, or a session of the nearby obedience class.

4. By now you may have decided which breeder you prefer. From here on the puppies will speak for themselves. One of them will pick you out, and that's it. However, if your heart can be guided by

Brood Bitch and Stud Dog competition at shows offers the opportunity for breeders to compare the finest of their litters against one another. The proud winner of the class at the Beverly Hills Kennel Club show on January 4, 1970, was Ch. Charlinore's Grand Ursula and her get owned and handled by Mrs. R. Wiggins. From left to right: Ch. Charlinore's Grand Ursula handled by Mrs. R. Wiggins, and Ursula's winning puppies: Patrichs Flaming Ember handled by Mr. R. Wiggins, Patrichs Forward Pass handled by Frank Aitken, Patrichs Fat Albert handled by Merry Prestidge.

194

Photo by William P. Gilbert

CH. SERENDIPITY'S PUSSY CAT seems as overjoyed as her breeder-owner-handler, Judith Goldworm. "Pussy Cat" had just won Best of Winners under judge John Stanek at the 1970 Westminster Kennel Club Show in New York.

Сн. Lorenz v. Liebiwil, (1963-1970) (Int. Ch. Anton v. Hofli ex Hulda v. Liebiwil), was owned by Dr. Antonio Morsiani of Italy and bred by Herr Paul Adam of Switzerland. Lorenz was a stud dog that stamped his puppies with his own excellent type as shown by his six-month-old offspring pictured below.

Rolando   Erla   Turk   Sultano   Rex

The Saint Puppy and His Parent

CH. SANCTUARY WOODS VANITY, a daughter of two champions, bred by Beatrice Knight and owned by Davy Hug. Here are four of her puppies, smooth and rough in the same litter. Left to right are HUGME'S FORTUNE COOKIE, smooth bitch, FRIENDLY NATURE and FINAL TOUCH, rough dogs, and FLARE FOR LUCK, smooth dog. They were sired by Ch. Sanctuary Woods You Lucky Boy. The width of a blaze does not ordinarily increase in proportion with head growth, therefore a puppy will seem to have a narrower blaze when he grows up.

your head, try to fall in love with the best pup in the litter. The breeder will have priced the litter members on his estimate of their quality. There won't be much difference in the prices, therefore the chances are that over the life of the dog, the highest-priced pup will cost you less and satisfy you more.

The ownership of a fine Saint Bernard puppy is a joy for all involved. A bit of advance preparation will make the experience more meaningful for everyone concerned.

197

What Does a Puppy Cost?

The first cost of a pup will be somewhere between three and ten per cent of his lifetime cost, but because it comes in one lump, puppy-pickers worry about it. Many of them, accustomed to buying commodities by the pound, assume that a large dog will naturally cost more than a small one. In fact, the cost of a purebred pup of any breed, quality for quality, will be about the same, whether the pup is a Chihuahua or a Saint Bernard.

There will be a wider price range between the good and poor specimens of any breed than among all breeds put together. The exception to this rule is that breed fashions change. There are always two or three breeds that are surging in popularity and become over-priced, then the cycle turns, supply exceeds demand, and the breeders can hardly give them away.

This phenomenon happened to the Saint Bernard in the late nineteenth century, when they became for a time the most numerous of all breeds, with the inevitable over-pricing and careless breeding. Fortunately this cycle happened long ago. The Saint's adaptability has made him a member of what society calls the "middle-class" family, of "medium" income, therefore the Saint Bernard pup is medium-priced and for the most part carefully bred, because the Saint-buying family wants to get its money's worth.

Obviously, if large pups and small pups sell for the same price, the Saint Bernard breeder is looking for love and exercise, not profit. As a practical matter, many of them defray the food bill by treating Saints as a hobby, then cut their dog-lover losses by raising a smaller breed as well.

What Does It Cost to Feed a Saint Bernard?

Whether you are sitting on the bench at a dog show, taking a walk in the woods, or dog-resting in your own living room, the first question asked of Saint fanciers is almost always, "What does it cost to feed your dog?" The Saint owner attempts to shrug off this impolite question by replying jocosely, "Less than Junior, here," or "About the same as me," or "Roughly a hundred miles to the gallon of milk."

The serious and correct answer is, "Less per pound of dog than any other dog." The Saint's metabolic rate is low, that is, he uses his

CH. APOLLO v. LION D'OR.

CH. SEVARG'S GINGER VON HEILMAN.

The two young champions above are both out of CH. HEILMAN's KATY VON GERO pictured elsewhere in this book. Their owners are Donald and Virginia Graves. The sire of "Ginger" was Heilman's Mark von Bornfeld. The sire of "Apollo" was Ch. Lion D'Or.

199

TYROL'S AL TORO V. JURI, seven-week smooth male (Canada). There is no substitute for experience. And, even experienced breeders make mistakes when grading puppies to keep or sell. Many breeders agree that if a puppy has good overall balance, generally correct anatomy at six to 12 weeks of age, and the head has the correct planes and a reasonable balance, a decision will be the best possible. One buys "potential" quality in young puppies.

TITAN'S FIGARO VON MALLEN, three-month rough male (U.S.A.). The muzzle is properly square of lip. The width is such that the muzzle fits smoothly into his cheek. His stop is abrupt with correct top skull structure. One can feel confident this puppy will develop into a highly typical adult. The Saint does not mature fully until the dog is three years old.

BRUNO DEL SOCCORSO, three-month-old rough male (Italy). "Bruno" is now an International Champion and looks almost identical in head as an adult as he did at this age. Puppies' ears seem to grow first and fastest. Then the muzzle starts to gain its length causing the head to seemingly "fall apart." Normally, if a puppy had a fine head to three months of age, he will regain proper type at maturity.

International CH. ANTON VON HOFLI, also pictured in profile earlier in the book. The editors use this view of this great dog to illustrate a dog in stance, totally unposed by a handler. When a dog is built right, he will stand correctly. "Anton's" legs dropped straight from his body (front and rear). The distance between his front and rear paws was equal. All four paws pointed straight forward. He was a perfectly balanced dog using "standard" ratios. The dog was 34 inches at the withers. His movement was of the finest. His rear and front angulation balanced at 45 degrees from horizontal. An interesting feature was his front assembly. He did not have the deep, full brisket extending between his front legs. "Anton" had a "running front"—much resembling the front assembly of a field dog. He was a tight, taut, muscular animal, totally masculine in every part. He died just before his tenth birthday in early 1970. Herr E. Bachmann (Switzerland) holds the lead.

201

CH. TITAN VON MALLEN (Ch. Lance's Robin Hood ex Phoebe von Mallen). owned and bred by Louis Mallen, is one of the most successful Saints of contemporary time. A multiple Specialty and Group winner, Titan has also sired a number of dogs that have become champions and made good wins of their own.

202

CH. EBENEZER VON MALLEN (Ch. Titan von Mallen ex Blanda v. Lanco), owned by Michael Alpert and bred by Robert Singer and J. F. McPartland.

fuel with economy. He is surpassed in this respect by the confined, domestic rabbit, who converts four pounds of food into one pound of rabbit. Next comes the pastured steer, who can make a pound of beef out of five pounds of hay. Among canines, the Saint wins, being able to convert six pounds of food into one pound of dog. Smaller canines have less favorable conversion rates, ranging all the way up to thirty pounds of food per pound of dog.

Once the Saint has his growth, his poundage intake will be about the same as yours. His metabolism rate is about the same as yours, and on the average he outweighs you, but he worries less than you do and works fewer hours in the day, so you break even on food intake.

The Saint breeder is almost always asked, "How much will he eat?" At this point the breeder, torn between his desire to state the fact and his desire to see you get a good puppy, mumbles something like, "Not much." He seldom dares remind you that through a growing period of several months the Saint puppy's body is geneti-

A far-away mood for a far-away Saint. "Beatrise" lives in Yugoslavia with her owner, Hana Bartosova.

cally conditioned to gain weight at the rate of a pound a day. If the conversion rate is six to one, the Saint puppy wants six pounds of food a day through this period, and from this food will produce the most dog for your money. Breeders ruefully point out that the ultimate bargain in dog-feeding, of course, is not to have a dog at all.

Will He Bite Me?

After, "How much does he eat?" The next question is usually, "Will he bite me?" The irresistible answer is, "Well, he's very fond of children." Other jocose answers run all the way from, "Probably not, sorry," through "Stick around and find out," to "Of course he will if you don't stop waving your fingers in his face."

Again the serious and correct answer is, "No, he won't, unless you give him a good reason." There are exceptions, but for the most part Saints are less inclined to violence than people.

The Saint Bernard Club of America awards the title "Top Stud Dog of the Year" to that male having the most champion get. For 1970 Ch. Saint's Retreat's Batman II (rough), won the official award. Batman was bred by Dr. George J. and Craig A. Wessar. He is owned by Charles E. Gamby & Dr. Wessar. Dr. Wessar, who is a licensed judge of the breed, is shown here handling Batman to a Best of Breed at the Ravenna Kennel Club under judge Marie A. Moore. By Ch. Lances Robin Hood, Top Sire of 1969 out of Saints Retreat's Royal Gigi.

BANZ v BACHING
6th generation

S.W.
DEEPTHOUGHT
6th generation

S.W. SINCERITY
5th generation

DEEP THOUGHT'S
ACE
5th generation

S.W. GULLIVER
4th generation

S.W. GULLIVER
4th generation

S.W.
FANTABULOUS
3rd generation

S.W. PICASSO
3rd generation

S.W. YOU LUCKY
BOY
2nd generation

S.W. VANITY
2nd generation

These photographs of dogs and their "get" for six generations will interest the student of Saint Bernard genetics. These straight ancestry selections are taken from the pedigree of *Ch. Sanctuary Woods Going My Way*, 1970 Saint Bernard Club of America's Specialty winner. The editors thank Mrs. Beatrice Knight and Mrs. Alvin Holt for accomplishing the pictorial research.

206

Does He Have a Good Disposition?

The correct answer is, "Not always, but usually better than mine." In the close relationship between dogs and people, a process of natural selection sees to it that the larger the dog, the better his disposition will probably be. Dog-owners will tolerate bad disposition in a small dog because he is physically easy to control. A Saint Bernard, somewhat heavier and far stronger than you are, simply has to have a good disposition in order to be tolerated by humans.

A bad disposition can occur by accident, or it can be forced upon any animal if the owner tries hard enough. Most dogs try to behave themselves because it's easier to get along with their owners if they do. Most Saint Bernards have good dispositions for the unromantic but effective reason that if they don't, they are big enough to be intolerable and their owners remove them from the genetic process.

Is the Saint a Good Watchdog?

The answer is "No," if by "watchdog" the questioner means an animal that will attack anybody on sight. Most Saints have excellent hearing and very acute scent. They have good memory for both friend and foe. Their outstanding trait seems to be an instinct for the preservation of life. Physical violence offends them, whether it be a cat killing a mouse, a fox killing a cat, two men striking each other, or even a parent spanking the baby. Given a soft-voiced and gentle burglar, a Saint would probably show him where the family silver is stored. However, the burglars do not know this. The Saint's impressive mass, musculature, and deep bass voice persuade the burglar to go burgle somebody else.

The family-raised Saint, allowed to become acquainted with postmen, milkmen, breadmen and meter readers, acquires a discrimination which helps him to distinguish between right and wrong, most of the time. This qualifies him as a babysitter, although he cannot change diapers or answer the telephone. If you seek a watchdog with some ability to evaluate, the Saint is unsurpassed.

When Should Training Begin?

The answer is, "Right now." A dog's life span is one-seventh of ours, but his growth, learning, and maturity rate in the early weeks is perhaps twenty times as fast. He wants to learn, up to the limit of his capacity, and he regards you as his teacher. He can be trained at any age, but the sooner the better, because the puppy likes and respects authority.

The Saint Bernard cannot be controlled by muscle power. He has more than you. He is controlled by his desire to please you. Your requirements are conveyed to him by words, which if you use consistently he can understand, and by means of a leash and collar. The training collar, erroneously called a "choke" collar, is a device by which you signal your intentions to the dog. No cruelty is involved. The eight-weeks-old puppy quickly learns to read your signals. The leash becomes a symbol of attention and play. When it appears the puppy knows he is going to have a good time. If, however, the Saint first feels leash and collar when he is eight months old, he may not be sure whether they represent fun or punishment.

How Can I Keep Him Out of Trouble?

There is one right answer, "A fenced yard." It is not a favor to the dog to let him run free. The fence establishes his boundary and his home. When he leaves this sanctuary to explore the world, he does so with you. The fence also improves his chances of survival, keeps him from becoming a town bum, and betters your relations with the neighbors.

The puppy will enjoy his personal fence more if it is established early in life. An older dog, with long memories of having roamed his own way, may regard the fence as confinement rather than possession.

The worst thing you can do to your Saint is put him on collar and chain, then leave him alone. Without a fence around him he is both tethered and vulnerable. This tends to make any dog belligerent. Leash and collar, with you in command, represent fun. A sizable fenced yard represents freedom and safety. A chain, without a human hand at the other end of it, represents dangerous slavery.

COLT FORTY-FIVE v. REAL GUSTO, C.D.X.
According to American Kennel Club regulations, "Colt" must jump his height at the shoulder (withers). This flying Saint finds 33½ inches of jump no problem at all. He lives in Pinckney, Michigan, with his proud owners, Mr. and Mrs. Thorne. In the words of his owner, Camilla, "A well trained dog is a pleasure to own."

Little Swiss Miss, aged 3, and Princess Margaret, aged 1, are headed north at a brisk trot. Owner Donald C. Little, of Rockwood, Michigan, is not pushing. He's trying to get aboard for a ride.

The Saint in Action

T HE Saint Bernard suffers from his own reputation. He is expected to be a draft animal, a house pet, a plaything and a workhorse. Pound for pound, he is presumed to be able to outpull any draft animal living, yet he is asked to run freely and gracefully when not under load. This is like asking a Percheron to dance the polka. The test of a good Saint is how well he can meet these varying demands.

In the following group of pictures you will observe a variety of gaits. Artists and photographers have done much work on the complexities of four-legged motion. Perhaps the earliest motion pictures were invented at the behest of a millionaire who wanted to prove that at certain moments a trotting horse has all four feet off the ground. A two-legged mammal is easy to observe. He has only two gaits, walk and run, the difference being that when he walks one foot is always on the ground. Four-legged mammals have a variety of gaits, among which the most common are called walk, trot, gallop, and pace.

The walk rhythm is "ca-lump ca-lump," with the left hind foot hitting the ground just before the right front foot, and just before

211

The dogs have just started a medium load, and are accelerating from walk into trot. Only the camera could detect that they are reaching almost, but not quite, in step.

Breaking into full working trot under light load, with the near back legs doing all the work at this instant. When the load is light, the dogs sometimes step off in parallel, rather than with opposite action.

Jarvis Hunt photos

212

A puppy and an adult, close relatives, and both walking. The puppy seems to be down in his pasterns, but in a few months' time he will have the same graceful movement as the adult. Photo study is by courtesy of Phyllis Jackson Smith, North Windham, Conn.

This is a rare exhibition of pace. The two far legs have just come down, and the near two are just lifting off. At full stretch in gait, the back lowers in the middle.

the left front foot lifts off. When walking, a dog always has three feet on the ground at any given instant.

Walk becomes trot when the rhythm is hastened, with the sequence of leg movements remaining the same. The sound now becomes "clump clump," because two feet are coming down and the other two lifting off at almost, though not quite, the same time. This is the action customarily referred to by dog fanciers as "gaiting."

A gallop is entirely different. The sound becomes "too-too-bum too-too-bum." With all four feet off the ground, the front two then strike in sequence, followed by the power stroke of the back two hitting the ground almost together. Puppies gallop before they trot, presumably because the coordination of the hind legs is not yet well developed. Almost any dog, in the excitement of play, will gallop to get from here to there.

Instead of trotting, some four-footed mammals prefer to pace. In this action the two right and two left legs work together. As in a trot, the sound is "clump clump," but made by two on a side rather than two on opposite sides. The feet cannot interfere with each

214

Heidi's Spice exhibits a slow trot, with two opposite feet firmly on the ground, and the other two coming forward. At this mid-point in gait, the back lifts in the middle.

other, therefore the animal does not have to move slightly sideways in order to keep from stepping on his own feet. However, the animal cannot pace slowly, because he depends on inertia to keep from falling over. Many dog show judges will reject a pacer as not "gaiting" properly, even though the pace at proper speed is the smoothest of all possible gaits, and allows the dog to run in a straight line.

As you will see, the purpose of his front legs is to hold him up, and the purpose of his back legs is to pull.

At a leisurely crossover from walk to trot, a Saint will go into a gait which horse fanciers call "singlefoot." In this gait two feet will be on the ground, one on each side and on the diagonal to each other. What happens next depends on how fast he wants to go, and how much load he is pulling. He will either drop back to a walk, with three feet on the ground, or move up to a trot, with one foot on the ground. No four-footed mammal will attempt to gallop under load unless he is unduly excited.

215

The St. Bernard Club of America National Specialty Show, 1972

THE DAY was May 26, 1972. The place was Peddler's Village, Lahaska, Pennsylvania. The event was the annual Specialty show of the Saint Bernard Club of America. On this day, at this place for this event would be assembled together the finest Saint Bernards from all over America. Canadian exhibitors and breeders were present, which gave the great show an international tone.

Peddler's Village lies in a valley between softly rolling hills. The bright spring sun lighted the day when 261 entries would be passed upon. Not just 261 Saint Bernard entries, but the finest assembly of the breed ever seen by Saint Fanciers.

To judge *The National* is, I am certain, a highlight in the life of any judge. To have a dog entered in the National is, in itself, an exciting event for each breeder and exhibitor. This annual show is where the most dedicated breeders and exhibitors bring their finest to demonstrate their progress in breeding for type and quality. To be asked to judge such a splendid array of animals is both a high compliment and a challenge of ability.

The membership of the Saint Bernard Club of America elected Mr. Herman A. Peabody and myself, E. Georgean Raulston, to pass

216

upon the entry. It was an awesome task that faced us that day—the responsibility and pressure to do all we could to point to true type and quality and, thereby, provide guidance for those seeking it.

Mr. Peabody will give his impressions, philosophy and judgments separate from mine. My assignment was All dogs and Intersex Competition. Mr. Peabody's assignment was All Female Classes.

The trophy table groaned under the weight of The Jay C. Gould Sterling Silver Punch Bowl; The Jacob Ruppert Sterling Silver Cup; The Harry Sangster Memorial Trophy; The Beatrice M. Knight Gratuity Trophy; as well as the beautiful Regular Class trophies which were provided for all placements. What a beautiful sight it was. The perfect weather, the beautiful location, a splendid array of silver trophies, two large rings—then my steward said, "It is 9:00 a.m., Mrs. Raulston, and we are ready to start."

How does that feel? Personally, I admit to a bit of stage fright as what seemed to be hundreds of people collected around my ring. Mostly, I felt deep and sincere responsibility. Many had come far, not only in miles but in years of trying to breed consistently better dogs. As I turned to start my assignment everything I had ever learned about the breed came forward and I knew I was ready. It was not an easy job in any class. Often, at smaller shows, one dog will stick out almost immediately as a quality animal: one with overall structural quality, breed type (massiveness), and near to the correct head as described in the standard. If the dog is moving well, you have found your first place and continue from there.

Not at this show. How proud the breeders and exhibitors must have been to see the great uniformity that is evolving within the breed. From East, West and Mid-West they came and with very few exceptions the dogs were showing "standardization." My heart swelled with pride for the devoted who had worked so hard to bring the breed to such beauty. Class after class they came until at one point it took all of my control to keep from going to the microphone and congratulating those present who were showing their dogs that day.

It was my responsibility to select from an entire ringful of excellent animals. The Open Dogs, Longhaired, Class was exceptional in that each dog conformed to the Standard to a high degree. What an incredible experience for me and, I am certain, all present. My professor under whom I studied in Europe was present, Mr. Albert de la

Sir Damon Lingenfelter, owned by Ron Mecale and Thomas Lingenfelter and bred by Mr. Lingenfelter, was Winners Dog and Best of Winners at the Specialty under Mrs. Raulston. He was handled by Robert J. Stebbins.

Ch. The Khan (left), owned by David Forrest was the winner of the Stud Dog Class at the Specialty under Mrs. Raulston. With him are his sons Mardonof's The Yankee Trader (center) handled by Mary Lou Dube and Highpoint's The Caliph (right) handled by Michael Alpert.

Rie. Mr. and Mrs. de la Rie had me in their home in Switzerland for three months while I apprenticed under this great "type" judge. After the judging, Mr. de la Rie agreed with me that nowhere in the world today could one see as many beautiful Saint Bernards collected together in one spot. No matter how far one had travelled, the show in its entirety was worth the effort. With so many beautiful dogs on display it was not a show but a Saint Bernard spectacular. No one had to feel badly about not placing where their dog could be considered "excellent." In my opinion, all of the dogs and puppies placed are potential champions. Further, there were many beautiful specimens who had to be left out of the ribbons who are potential champions. While I could not acknowledge them with ribbons that day, I do it now.

My Winners Dog was from the Open Dogs, Longhaired Class: Sir Damon Lingenfelter, bred by Tom Lingenfelter. How one selects a fine animal from an entire ring of fine animals probably goes beyond knowledge of the Standard, a thorough study of head type and overall type, quality of structure, movement, etc. When I looked at that beautiful ring of class winners I felt my job was impossible. Each one was so beautiful. I especially recall that great puppy, Emir of Highpoint. In my opinion, they should all have had points that day. Then, as I recalled faults of each, strengths and value of each, something came to my mind: "Massive, male-looking." Surely they were all that, but one stood out as "MALE" to me at that moment and I pointed to him without further thought. I have never doubted my opinion at that moment was entirely correct.

It has always been interesting to me that the majority of dogs I put up end up being highly prepotent studs. Perhaps that, in the final analysis is what instinct speaks for among a group of highly equal animals. The purpose of showing is to prove the animal worthy of being bred. Each dog is placed against the Standard individually and then compared against the group with which he is being judged. Where a dog fits the standard to a high degree, has nobility, style, and stands out in his class as being 100% masculine, massive and strong—well, in this show it gave Sir Damon Lingenfelter a five point major and Best of Winners.

The Best of Breed Class. What can I say of that magnificent collection of Saint Bernards? It was a show in itself, and it was an

Loconte photo

Ch. Titan von Mallen, bred and owned by Louis Mallen, is shown winning Best of Breed in an entry of 261 at the Saint Bernard Club of America's 1972 Specialty under the author, E. Georgean Raulston. Mr. Mallen is handling here. Mrs. Marian Sharp, Show Secretary and Mr. Fred Anderson, President of the Saint Bernard Club of America present the trophies.

enormous compliment in itself. As I stood in the center of the ring feasting my eyes on beautiful dog after beautiful dog I felt a little sad that only one could be Best of Breed. So many deserve mention. All of my favorites were there from shows I had judged during the preceding two years. I wanted to speak to the breed through my judging and say, "In my opinion the dog I select from this ring of dogs is what I feel should set the prototype." Not one dog was faultless. All were beautiful. I do not admire judgements that see only faults. One must train the eye for beauty. There will always be a

Francis photo

Ch. Sanctuary Woods Kleona, owned by Robert E. and Mary L. Tarlton and bred by Beatrice M. Knight, was Best of Opposite Sex at the National Specialty under Mrs. Raulston. She is shown in a subsequent triumph taking Best of Opposite Sex at the Saint Bernard Club of the Pacific Coast under the celebrated Swiss authority Mr. Albert de la Rie. Kleona's breeder, Mrs. Knight handled her to the win.

fault or two or some small flaw in the symmetry or balance on even the greatest dog.

There were excellent dogs around me to the number of 38. From that number I had to eliminate 37 and find the one against which all others could be matched and found lacking to some degree—small though it was in many cases. That dog, in that ring that day would then, in my opinion, be the archtype. I finally eliminated all but four Saint Bernards: Ch. Titan Von Mallen, Ch. Vedalyn Prinz Luis' von Mallen, Ch. Rembrandt von Mallen, and Ch. The Kahn.

Among bitches I found Ch. Sanctuary Woods Kleona, Ch. Madonna's Heidi, Ch. Serendipity's Pussycat, and Ch. Ursula von Mallen. All were superb specimens. In a moment of judgment I pulled out Ch. Titan von Mallen, Ch. Vedalyn Prinz Luis' von Mallen, and Ch. Rembrant von Mallen. My final decision was for the enormously splendid specimen, Ch. Titan von Mallen. After I selected my Best of Winners, I turned my attention to another difficult decision, Best of Opposite Sex. It finally came down to two bitches and then, after final comparison, I selected the beautiful bitch, Ch. Sanctuary Woods Kleona for Best of Opposite Sex to Best of Breed.

It was a day the exhibitors and breeders could be proud of. It was their show, their dogs, their hard work on display to prove breed progress. I was honored that the majority had enough confidence in my judgment to have me. My heart is with the breed and the breed has never looked so beautiful en masse or individually. My congratulations.

Impressions of the 1972 Specialty of the Saint Bernard Club of America

by Herman A. Peabody

Having been honored with being chosen to judge the bitch classes at the 1972 National Specialty of the Saint Bernard Club of America I feel that some reflections on the dogs I judged there might be appeciated.

After judging the Parent Specialty I realize more fully that the National is not just another dog show. Those who show at the National are presenting their very finest specimens and in the best possible manner and condition. For any lover of the breed it is a profoundly thrilling experience to see so many of the world's finest Saints gathered for this great annual event. For the judge such an assembly to pass on is both gratifying and frustrating—gratifying because it shows that the fancy hold's the judge's opinion in high regard to select him to judge at a Parent Specialty and frustrating because with a whole ringful of quality animals there are only four ribbons that can be awarded in any one class.

222

Loconte photo
Snobelt's Rosé of Dereworth, owned by Michael Tuite and William Dunn and bred by Suzanne and Michael Tuite, was Winners Bitch at the 1972 Saint Bernard Club of America Specialty under Mr. Herman A. Peabody. Suzanne M. Tuite handled her to the win.

The quality of the dogs at the National was sufficient to prove to even the most skeptical that our breed is going forward in spite of the current upsurge in popularity it is now experiencing.

My own personal contact with the breed as a breeder, exhibitor and judge goes back many years. I had my first Saints during the '40's and by the quality seen in the dogs shown today those were pretty poor specimens. I have personally witnessed many changes occur in the Saint Bernard over the years and it pleases me to report that Saints being produced today are a vast improvement over what

223

has been bred in the past. I have seen the fruits of the efforts of sincere and dedicated Saint breeders. Drooping eyelids, hound ears, masses of freckles and foul temperament are rarely, if ever, seen in the show ring today. Poor temperament was particularly prevalent during the forties and fifties and was responsible for giving our breed a bad name in some areas. Happily, temperament and conformation have improved together.

In closing, let me repeat that in my opinion the quality of the dogs shown at the 1972 National Specialty was of more uniformly good type, soundness, temperament, coat quality and coloring and they were generally better conditioned, groomed and presented than any group of Saint Bernards I have ever judged or observed at any show. It was, beyond a doubt, the Saint fancy's finest hour in the United States.